SUPPER

recipes worth staying in for

FLORA SHEDDEN

For James – I look forward to eating many
more feasts with you

and

For Gramps – who was one of my
favourite people to feed

SUPPER

recipes worth staying in for

FLORA SHEDDEN

photography by Laura Edwards

Hardie Grant

BOOKS

Introduction

Supper, Dinner, Tea, Feast ... Frankly, who cares what you call it?
We all end our day with a meal.

All these words have so many different connotations and associations.
'Supper' translates in my mind as a more relaxed evening meal. This is
partly to do with the rise of supper clubs hosted in people's houses, using
whatever plates, chairs and cutlery they can get their hands on. I see it as an
event that can happen daily with little pressure or fuss. 'Dinner' is its formal
equivalent, the sort that involves hosting and entertaining and maybe even
bringing out the fancy glasses. For many people, dinner can also mean
lunch, something that will always wholly confuse me. 'Tea' is what we ate at
home as kids. A very monotone chorus of 'what's for tea?' would start in our
house at around 4 p.m., when we got back from school, and probably didn't
stop until we were faced with a plate of pasta a few hours later. So, what
do you call the in-between? The sort of meal you have spent time over, no
matter how much or how little. A meal that is enjoyed at your kitchen table
with candles and perhaps maybe even a napkin, but with no formalities
or logistics to consider. Just those you spend most of your time with.
I settled for 'supper', which I think finds the perfect balance of casual and
considered dining. Supper to me is the most pleasurable and relaxed form
of eating. But in a world where lunch can be called dinner, you should by all
means name it what you like.

Ultimately, it doesn't really matter what you name your evening meal.
In our unbelievably busy lives, the work-life balancing act and constant
demands of day-to-day, dinners are getting harder and harder to find time
and energy for. These days, we have access to amazing (and lots of not-so-
amazing) meals right at our fingertips, many that will be brought right
to our door. When motivation is lacking, all too often the temptations of
modern-day life take over. Dinners and the art of dining in can easily be
lost among the hustle and bustle. I have been hugely guilty of this myself.

Convenience (and sadly often highly processed) food after an exceptionally long day of cooking for other people is horribly easy to fall back on.

For me, cooking should be something to look forward to at the end of the day – a reward or a tasty form of compensation for making it through a particularly difficult one, or a celebration of a day well spent.

During various lockdowns in recent years, the world became a little quieter. We stayed at home, tried to look after ourselves as best we could and became inventive with what we could cook, now that takeaways and ready meals felt unnecessary and unaffordable for many. This wave of quiet made me fall in love with dining in all over again.

I have long been a fan of entertaining and cooking for crowds. I cook for and serve hundreds of people daily in my bakery and even wrote a book on cooking for big gatherings. But with both of those things out of the question in lockdown I returned to cooking, and taking my time over cooking, for those I loved the most. This is how I started spending time in the kitchen, and how I first came to adore it. I cooked for my siblings and my parents – the people I spent most of my days with. It was a gentle form of therapy to return to doing this again after some very hectic years. What, when and how we eat can completely turn our days and our mindset around.

THE JOY OF DINING IN

The aim of this book is to spark or reignite our love of cooking at home. I hope it is an approachable and helpful guide to dining at home, no matter the day, the occasion or the meal.

Eating supper happens 7 days a week, 52 weeks a year. We do this to look after ourselves and those we love. It is essential. And yet so often the effort and pleasure that come from taking the time to cook and sitting down to eat at a table is reserved for formal occasions, reasons to celebrate or hosting people. The rest of the time there is often a sense of the mundane about evening meals. I hope this book encourages you to dedicate the time to slicing some garlic, looking out for serving platters and nice glasses, and rummaging through cupboards for forgotten ingredients. Even if you only have 20 minutes, use them to cook and then take the time again to eat – deadlines can wait. There are recipes both fast and slow in here, some more effortless than others, but all of them taste a heck of a lot better when eaten at a table with those you love. And who cares if the table is covered with letters, stray belongings and other signs of life?

Eating around a table is something I grew up with. I didn't take it for granted but it really surprised me how hard it is to maintain for two people. Before I moved in with my partner James, I was used to five people around a table noisily chatting, often arguing, sometimes wolfing down food, and sometimes pushing it around the plate. When there are just two of you, it becomes easy to eat standing up in the kitchen, or with a plate balanced on your crossed legs in front of the telly. We do still do this from time to time, but our aim is to spend more nights of the week at a table than eating in a pool of blue television light. To combat this, we started a weekly dinner where we would cook, talk, and most importantly eat at the table.

I can't quite remember the exact process of planning our first menu. I think I went into a shop with a list of ingredients and failed to source any of them. The resulting menu wasn't quite what I had in mind, but I was excited all the same. We started with gin and tonics while cooking, nearly set off the smoke alarm crisping up some duck, ate plenty of dauphinois potatoes, fried cavolo nero with a green sauce and some hazelnuts, drank lots of wine, played a game of chess, and then tucked into a chocolate cremaux with brandy-soaked cherries. I had set the table with a stripy blue-and-white tablecloth, used some little blue-and-gold drinking glasses I inherited from my granny, white linen napkins I had bought for a supper club hosted some years ago (un-ironed, always, much to my mother's horror), and plenty of candles from my excessive and until-now unused collection. We didn't have any flowers because Scotland in January is not famed for its blooms. I was quite drunk by the time we went to bed and left

SUPPER

almost all the clearing up for the morning. It was heaven, despite the fact that I was so chronically terrible at chess. I think at some point during the evening I said we should do it every week, before waking up six hours later with a headache only red wine can cause.

Surprisingly, we did do it every week, in one form or another, and it became our Friday Feast.

As time went on, Friday Feast has changed and altered. Life became busy again and occasionally it would take the form of a takeaway, but this time sat at the table, plates, cutlery and napkins all set out, candles lit and flowers arranged. Our quick go-to midweek meals started to become occasions in themselves, too. We would sit at the table, still half covered with the chaos and clutter that accompanies life, and perhaps we would even light a candle leftover from a weekend feast before. And, of course, there are still TV dinners and meals eaten straight from the pan, from time to time, but for the most part we have returned to our dining table.

Until lockdown, it hadn't even dawned on me to make as much of an effort for eating at home as I would if I was entertaining. I would never have set the table with tealights, multiple glasses and napkins for just the two of us before. But I did and I have loved it ever since. When I do go all out and set the table fully, it feels like a private party. We eat when and how we want, wearing what we want and still it feels sociable and special. I have sat down to a candlelit dinner in my pyjamas on numerous occasions. This flexibility is what makes me enjoy dining at home more than anything else. You need to be flexible to cook well. Supper will be ready when it's good and done and your stress levels will be all the better for it.

RECLAIMING THE DINING TABLE

Our dining tables have changed enormously over the past few years. They have been transformed into desk spaces, work from home set-ups, home schooling Zoom stations, small business HQs, sourdough and banana bread production lines, to name but a few. Our dining table is often littered with letters, documents, Z reports from the bakery, mail, laundry bags, and all the other paraphernalia that comes from working at (or in my case right below) home. It's nearly impossible to motivate creating a dining experience when work and life are so intertwined.

Friday Feast, for us, was a way to reclaim our dining table for what it ought to be, even if that does just mean condensing the clutter to one end, half sorting it as you go. Clearing space on the table works wonders when it comes to feeling inspired in the kitchen. I try to do it before I even start cooking. That is the wonderful thing about dining tables. They are so versatile and can be transformed repeatedly throughout the day, even if it is just quick reshuffles, like costume changes backstage.

THE ART OF COOKING SUPPER AT HOME

A few people have commented on how small my kitchen at home is. I think when you cook for a living people expect a large space with plenty of work surfaces, cupboards and multiple ovens (I would kill for multiple ovens). In our professional kitchen we are very lucky and do have these things, but the irony is that all my writing and testing, for both the business and my books, is done in our small domestic kitchen.

The kitchen takes up just under half of our L-shaped dining room and is laid out as a horseshoe with the oven and hob on the left-hand side, sink in the middle and refrigerator on the right. It has very little usable work surface and normally there's someone standing right in front of the drawer you want to access (James). One door has fallen off so many times we have simply got rid of it. We have a grand total of four cupboards and four drawers for storage and a washing machine so aggressive you need to move dishes from the draining board above to prevent any breakages. It is a disjointed sort of space to both work and live in, and I don't think I am alone when it comes to cooking in awkward spaces. I suspect the vast majority of us do so. Surely even the best-designed kitchens and spaces must have one form of nuisance? Even if it is simply that a soft-close door doesn't slam in a moment of rage with quite the effect you wanted it to.

I think we all get used to these little irritating traits in our houses, learning how we work with our kitchens and their individual ticks. Often this means we can cook an abundance of dishes in our 'small' kitchens better and more effortlessly than anyone else. I have spent great chunks of time getting to know and often fighting with our wee kitchen and this at long last has been rewarded with a small sense of rhythm.

Cooking at home should be a relaxed affair and so the same applies to these recipes. They are simply suggestions for you to use and abuse to your heart's content, and adapt to your own kitchen and rhythm. The results will be no better than the quality of ingredients you are using, so it is far better to substitute an element of the dish with something lovingly produced or grown than to use something out of season (and therefore sub-par and flavourless) just because the recipe says so.

I have learned far more about cooking when feeding those I live with than when trying to please others. If a dish doesn't work out, there is no disappointment from guests or self-criticism. You can change tactic and serve something quick, like a plate of silky scrambled eggs on toast dripping with butter, and it doesn't matter. To cook with that amount of freedom is the best way to learn anything, I find. If it does work, even better, but putting the outcome aside you have managed to gather and feed those you love.

Ultimately, this is a collection of things I like to cook for the people that are closest to me. You can use these recipes in whatever way you fancy. By all means adapt them to feed 24 people, eat them in front of the telly if it's what you wish to do, or change it up to serve them at other times of the day for lunch or breakfast. They are yours with which to do as you wish, but I really hope that – at least once – they make you want to set the table, light some candles, and have supper with those you may not normally be trying to impress.

With love,
Flora

November 2021

Using this book

HOW TO FEAST

The (somewhat sad) reality is that you cannot feast in the traditional sense every night. Time, money, energy, waistlines, and all the other boring elements of day-to-day life must come into play here and ultimately even I can admit that it is an unsustainable thing to achieve night on night. And so, this leaves evenings where speed is called for, or something light and quick. I hope these chapters help to cater for both of these conundrums – bountiful meals and food for eating in a hurry. I also hope you are able to adapt the different recipes and pair them off to create your own feasts. There are some midweek menus that will allow you to feast fast, along with long meandering meals that allow you to slow down and take your time over many dishes.

Although the connotations of feasting are grand, elaborate meals, I hope this book demonstrates that a feast can be made up of two quick dishes, an excellent drink, a few candles, and a napkin or two. It all counts and should feel bountiful regardless of what is or isn't on the table.

HOW TO PULL TOGETHER A MENU

Menu is perhaps an elaborate term for what this book is all about, but honestly I cannot think of a better one. And even though your menus aren't printed on little A5 pieces of natural paper (do this if you feel the desire to), I suppose when coming up with a feast you must consider the same principles as those required for menu writing.

I have featured various options for menus throughout this book, which I hope will help and encourage you into the kitchen, however I thought it was important to explain the process I go about to get there. A huge part of my cooking and feasting style comes from looking at different cookbooks and pairing off recipes that I think would complement and balance each other regardless of where they came from. Playing matchmaker with different

food writers is one of the most inspiring things you can do as a cook
and always helps me break out of any culinary-based rut I find myself in.
Coordinating recipes based on their hands-on involvement, ingredients
and serving style is a lot easier than it sounds and for me is the best way to
generate excitement in the kitchen. On this basis, I hope the tips on the
following pages help you to pull your own menus together when perusing
one or one hundred different cookbooks, websites, or crumpled newspaper
cuttings, or simply give you permission to play around with and edit mine –
it would be an honour.

MARRYING INGREDIENTS

I was serious when I said it was a job all about matchmaking. First, and
most importantly, when I create a menu I begin with a 'hero' recipe. This
is the starting point that will lead to all other dishes. From this hero recipe
I choose the main or most crucial ingredient and pair it up with two other
ingredients that complement the hero one. The key things to consider
during this process are:

Seasonality – probably the most crucial part to consider. What time of year
are you cooking? Choose ingredients that are at their peak at that time. For
example, do not choose strawberries in the middle of winter even if you
think they will go brilliantly with a pistachio cake. They will only be
brilliant with said cake when they are at their best in the height of summer,
and not when they are sad and a little bit sour during the darker months
(I suppose we can all get like this in the depths of winter).

Flavour – this can be a little more complex as it is down to personal
preference. You might like sweet and salty foods to be paired off, or sour
and sticky. My main goal here is to always include something fresh or
vibrant enough to act as a bit of a palette cleanser. The biggest mistake you
can make is to serve lots of strong or rich dishes together, as this ultimately
means all the flavours will be fighting. Background and subtle flavours are
your friend and something that should not be overlooked.

Texture – a menu should have a variety of textures in it, simply to keep people interested in the meal. There is a reason why people who juice everything look so miserable.

Colour – a colour theme for recipes is a horrible idea, sorry. As the old cliché goes: we eat with our eyes. A variety of colours helps this enormously. By all means coordinate your table dressings, but nothing is quite as unappetising as various dishes all resembling almost exactly the same shade.

Who you are cooking for – it's annoying, but I suppose it is good to think of others from time to time.

What do you want to cook and eat yourself – although I have placed your own considerations last, it is important to listen to yourself on this point. Even if you know a delicious fresh cucumber salad would pair nicely with some gingery noodles, those noodles will taste not half as good as they should if your heart isn't in it.

COOKING

It is important to consider how everything needs to be cooked, prepped and stored. If you are the make-ahead sort, you should consider this when seeking out recipes and check that they are suitable to prepare ahead of time. What you don't want is multiple recipes that all need a lot of work right before serving. One dish that requires a bit of last-minute attention is fine, but the juggle to do three like that can turn the air blue. Try to seek out recipes that have a variety of prep requirements so you can delegate time easily and without flap. It is also important to make sure you have plenty of oven or refrigerator space, so read recipe methods for length of oven/hob time, oven temperatures and chilling methods (if required) and make sure they don't clash, e.g. meringues (a low oven temperature) will not be friends with roasted chicken (a high oven temperature), so are best made ahead of time or the day before.

ON THE TABLE

It sounds silly but I always consider how dishes will look and be displayed on the table when putting together a meal. You don't, for example, want to serve multiple dishes that look similar in terms of texture and colour. I also like to think about what dishes will be served in – is it an oven-to-table dish that can be served in the roasting pan or tray (make sure you have a mat for this) or will I be plating and garnishing a dish to go on the table? It is at this stage that I like to think about decoration, candles and all the other faffy bits I adore so much. Matching coloured candlesticks with flowers is great fun, but it is also a joy when you can tie them into your food. If you are cooking a vibrant spinach and bulgur wheat dish, it would be rude not to grab some green foliage or napkins.

If I am being truly honest, I have occasionally decided on recipes based entirely on ceramics, vases or flowers I have prepared beforehand (blood-orange Turkish delight served on a plate glazed in pale pink is frankly delightful). This route can also work for the menu writer as obsessed with colours as I am, but it is important you consider the other points above at the same time.

EATING

How and when you will eat should also be considered. If you are eating al fresco with limited table or lap space, remember this before choosing a recipe that involves a heavy amount of cutlery work or large plates in order to enjoy it. The same applies to any recipes that require specialist equipment or serving dishes. It doesn't mean you shouldn't do it, but you should bear this in mind and consider ways to overcome it, e.g. hammers for tricky shellfish claws; espresso cups, mugs or small tumblers in place of ramekins or pudding moulds; sticks soaked in water instead of kebab skewers (olive branches have saved me before). Most things can be adapted to suit what you have already, but it is worth planning ahead.

Time of night should also be considered both for menu and atmosphere. If you are eating on a hot evening in the middle of summer, it would be a fair guess that you won't want a large joint of roasted meat, and probably likely you won't need quite as many tealights. Equally, a salad followed by ice cream might also be unappealing in January when your body weight is approximately 42% wool. On these darker nights, you can light as many candles as you wish!

NOTES ON THE RECIPES

All oven temperatures are for a fan oven.

All lemons are unwaxed.

All yoghurt is full-fat Greek yoghurt.

All tinned tomatoes are peeled plum, preferably San Marzano.

All milk is whole (full-fat) milk.

I use two types of olive oil: a light plain oil for cooking, and a fruiter extra virgin for dressing and finishing dishes. It is really important not to replace one with the other.

All salt is Maldon flaky sea salt unless otherwise stated.

All eggs are large and free-range. If you only have smaller eggs, work on the basis that a large egg weighs roughly 50–60 g (2¼ oz) when cracked.

All stock used is either homemade, high quality fresh stock or using stock cubes. When using stock cubes simply follow the packet instruction. For smaller quantities of stock e.g. 200 g (7 oz) I tend to just use half a stock cube.

All liquids are measured by weight for multiple reasons: accuracy, preventing any waste (when decanting from a measuring jug to a mixing bowl/pan) and most helpfully to limit the amount of washing up. If you

aren't as sold on the concept of weighing your liquids, simply work
to the below approximate formula, but bear in mind that it is hard to
be exact with such conversions, as temperature and brand types can
alter the result:

– water, stock, alcohol, milk, citrus and fruit juice, and vinegars are like for
   like in weight and volume: 100 g = 100 ml

– double (heavy) cream weighs a small amount less in volume: 94 g = 100 ml

– golden syrup and honey both weigh more than their volume: 145 g = 100 ml

– most oils weigh a little less than their volume: 95 g = 100 ml

Portions sizes do vary in this book. In the 'Thirty-minute tea' and 'In a
hurry' chapters, the recipes are designed to be brought together quickly and
without too much thought and this naturally translates as fairly standard
portions with not much in the way of leftovers. In the 'Candlelight' and
'Sweet endings' chapters, the recipes require effort and care and often
are easier and more economical to cook in larger quantities. This is my
favourite type of cooking as your effort is rewarded with plenty of food
to feast on again the following night (Saturday meals post Friday Feast
have become a joy in our house). If you know you won't manage to eat
your leftovers the following day, I encourage you to either freeze them the
next morning in order to avoid anything getting forgotten about in the
back of the refrigerator or alternatively consult the 'Let's do it all again'
chapter. There are various ideas for working with leftovers and extras here,
and alongside considering sustainability with food, who wouldn't want to
create a whole new feast? I also think it's apt to note the old saying about
how you always cook for the amount of people you grew up with. I was in
a household of five and no matter how much knowledge or experience I
have, I will always end up cooking for five. At least it means we always get to
enjoy leftovers.

Please source your ingredients as thoughtfully as possible. A U.S. wartime
poster advocated that you should cook your food with care, buy locally, serve

just enough, and use what is left. 'Do not waste it!' This still rings true a century later and is important to keep at the forefront of your mind when shopping. Try to avoid foods with high air miles (consult packaging regularly for this) and where possible shop for loose fruit and vegetables that are seasonal and sustainably grown. Always aim for high-welfare meats and dairy products. It is also important to try to avoid overly processed foods and products, as it is nearly impossible to trace every ingredient and its origin. It is a minefield when shopping at the moment and no one will ever get it 100% right, so don't be harsh on yourself.

NOTES ON SUBSTITUTES

I have added tried and tested substitutes to the bottom of each recipe for two reasons:

Firstly, I hope it encourages you to adapt and change recipes as you go and inspires you to look at seasonality and locality when cooking from this book. This is even more important when pulling together full menus, as you might find two recipes that would be delicious together but alas one ingredient from each dish is not in season at the same time as the other. I hope the substitutes will help with any alterations to overcome this problem, and make the recipes feel relaxed enough for you to run with them in whatever shape or form you fancy.

Secondly, I hope it prevents too much waste. All too often with recipe books, people find one recipe they are keen to try and head off the shops to buy all the ingredients on the list. Hopefully, the substitutions will remind you of the slightly sad broccoli sitting in the bottom of your veg drawer, or the herbs that are in desperate need of being used somewhere. Always try to shop in your own home for a recipe before heading out.

CHAPTER ONE

In a
hurry

Chickpea *and* Shallot Orecchiette

Serves 4

a little olive oil

2 shallots, finely sliced

4 garlic cloves, finely sliced

5 g (¼ oz) thyme

2 tsps cumin seeds

200 g (7 oz) orecchiette
  pasta

1 × 400 g (14 oz) tin
  chickpeas (garbanzo
  beans)

juice of 1 lemon

10 g (½ oz) flat-leaf parsley,
  finely chopped

200 g (7 oz/scant 1 cup)
  vegetable or chicken
  stock

salt and freshly ground
  black pepper

grated Parmesan, to serve

SUBS

shallots – red onions

thyme – marjoram;
  rosemary

orecchiette – macaroni;
  farfalle

I suppose this can fall into the category of a warm salad, but I enjoy it equally as much when cold. I simply add in lots more chopped herbs once cooled down and a little olive oil to loosen. You can also enjoy this almost as a stew-type creation – add in some more stock and cook the pasta until a little underdone before adding to the pan. A truly versatile dish!

In a large, shallow pan, heat a little oil over a medium heat, add the shallots and garlic and cook until softened. Pick the thyme leaves and add to the pan along with the stalks (you can fish them out later). Add the cumin seeds and continue to cook for a few minutes.

Meanwhile, boil the kettle, then pour plenty of the boiling water into a large saucepan. Add the pasta and a generous pinch of salt and cook for about 8 minutes or until al dente.

While the pasta is cooking, add the drained chickpeas and lemon juice to the onion pan. Cook for a few moments more, then season with salt and pepper and add the parsley and the stock.

Drain the pasta, reserving some of the cooking water. Add the pasta to the pan with the sauce, cook for a minute or two and add some of the starchy pasta water to loosen if needed.

Serve immediately with a generous amount of grated Parmesan on top.

Courgette *and* Lemon Pasta *with* Almonds

Serves 2

125 g (4 oz) wholewheat
   spaghetti or bucatini
a generous glug of olive oil
75 g (2½ oz) unsalted butter
350 g (12 oz) courgettes
   (zucchini), finely sliced
4 garlic cloves, finely sliced
75 g (2½ oz/5 tbsps) white
   wine
zest and juice of ½ lemon
small handful of fresh
   oregano, leaves picked
25 g (¾ oz) flat-leaf parsley,
   stalks and all, finely
   chopped
45 g (1¾ oz/½ cup) finely
   grated Parmesan
45 g (1¾ oz/½ cup) flaked
   (slivered) almonds,
   toasted
salt and freshly ground
   black pepper

SUBS
white wine – chicken or veg
   stock
parsley – mint; chives
almonds – toasted walnuts;
   pumpkin seeds

When I was wee, my mum would regularly buy wholewheat pasta (a rarity at the time) for us from a health shop. I think I am phrasing it politely when I say we did not like it. Twenty years later, wholewheat pasta has come on leaps and bounds and I have come to love its almost nutty flavour.

Bring a large pan of salted water to the boil, then add the pasta and cook for 7–8 minutes or until al dente.

Meanwhile, heat the oil and a small knob of the butter in a large frying pan (skillet) over a medium-high heat until melted. Add the courgettes and garlic and cook down until softened and beginning to colour slightly. Add a splash of white wine to the pan and cook for a further 2–3 minutes. Add the lemon juice and zest and continue to cook for a few more minutes, then season lightly.

When the pasta is cooked, drain, reserving some of the cooking water.

Add the pasta to the courgette pan along with the oregano leaves, finely chopped parsley and the remaining butter. Remove from the heat and loosen with a splash of the cooking water if required. Finish by mixing through the most of the Parmesan and season again to taste.

Serve immediately, garnished with the flaked almonds, a little more Parmesan and some black pepper.

Halloumi, Melon *and* Tomato Salad *with* Chilli

Serves 2 as a main or 4 as a side

250 g (9 oz) heritage tomatoes or mixed cherry tomatoes
100 g (3½ oz) halloumi
¼ tsp chilli (hot pepper) flakes
1 small gala or cantaloupe melon
5 g (¼ oz) mint leaves
1 tbsp lime juice
2 tbsps olive oil
1 tsp honey
salt and freshly ground black pepper

SUBS
halloumi – feta
mint – flat-leaf parsley
honey – maple syrup; agave syrup

This recipe began life in Aran, the bakery I own and live above. It has featured on our mid-summer salad counter for over three years and has always proved popular. It's too good to just keep it for lunchtime – it makes for a perfect light meal on a hot summer's night (not that we get many of those in Scotland). I like to eat it with slices of sourdough, drizzled with olive oil and salt, and baked in the oven for 5 minutes.

Roughly chop the tomatoes and add to a bowl. Crumble the halloumi with your hands and mix into the tomatoes along with the chilli flakes. Cut the melon into large chunks, then finely slice the mint leaves and add both to the bowl.

Whisk together the lime juice, oil and honey until smooth, then season lightly. Toss through the salad and add more black pepper to taste.

Serve immediately.

Cauliflower, Celery
and Hazelnuts

Serves 2 as a main or 4 as a side

FOR ROASTING THE CAULIFLOWER
1 medium cauliflower
1 tsp ground coriander
1 tsp za'atar
1 tsp salt
a few cracks of freshly ground black pepper
2 tbsps olive oil

TO FINISH
20 g (¾ oz/2 generous tbsps) hazelnuts
5 g (¼ oz) fresh coriander (cilantro)
½ celery stalk
40 g (1½ oz/scant 3 tbsps) olive oil
40 g (1½ oz/scant 3 tbsps) milk (or double/heavy cream)
seeds from ¼ pomegranate
salt and freshly ground black pepper

SUBS
za'atar – ½ tsp dried thyme mixed with ½ tsp sesame; sumac
milk – oat milk; cream
hazelnuts – almonds

I was pretty slow to join the cauliflower appreciation club, but at last I am now a fully fledged member. Although I won't be rushing to make 'cauliflower pizzas' anytime soon, I am endlessly impressed with its versatility.

Preheat the oven to 220°C fan (475°F/gas 9).

Roughly chop the cauliflower: stalk, leaves and all (the smaller the pieces, the quicker it will cook). Reserve a few florets for garnishing. Add to a baking tray (pan) along with the spices, 1 tsp of salt, some black pepper and the 2 tbsps of oil, then toss together. Roast in the oven for 10–15 minutes.

Meanwhile, toast the hazelnuts, either in a dry frying pan (skillet) or in the oven for 5 minutes. Crush them roughly in a pestle and mortar. Pick half of the coriander leaves and finely chop the rest. Finely slice the reserved cauliflower florets and the celery.

Place roughly half of the roasted cauliflower (use the roasted stalks for this, not the leaves) into a food processor along with the oil and milk. Blitz until smooth, then check for seasoning.

Spoon the puréed cauliflower onto your serving plate/s using the back of a spoon to swirl it in a circle. Cover with the chopped coriander and half of the pomegranate seeds. Next, arrange the remaining roasted cauliflower over the top, making sure you can still see a little of the purée at the edges. Sprinkle with half of the hazelnuts. Place the celery and raw cauliflower slices in among the dish, then finally garnish with the picked coriander leaves, and the remaining pomegranate seeds and hazelnuts. Serve warm or at room temperature.

SOUPS FOR SUPPER

CAULIFLOWER AND MUSTARD

Serves 4–6

1 large cauliflower
2 small banana shallots
½ fennel bulb
1 apple
1 tsp cumin seeds
1 tsp brown mustard seeds
olive oil, for drizzling
about 1 kg (2 lb 4 oz/4 cups)
   vegetable stock
salt and freshly ground black pepper

TO SERVE
toasted cumin seeds
toasted sunflower seeds
coriander (cilantro) sprigs

Preheat the oven to 220°C fan (475°F/ gas 9). Roughly chop the whole cauliflower, then place on a baking tray (pan). Finely slice the shallots, fennel and apple and add to the tray. Add the spices and season. Drizzle with oil and mix together. Roast for 20 minutes or until everything is soft and beginning to colour.

In a large saucepan, bring the stock to the boil. Add the roasted veggies and boil for 5 minutes. Blend the soup until smooth using a food processor or stick blender. Loosen with a little stock, and serve drizzled with some oil, the cumin and sunflower seeds, and coriander.

FENNEL, LEEK AND POTATO

Serves 4–6

1 medium white onion
1 leek
2 fennel bulbs, fronds reserved for garnish
2 thyme sprigs
olive oil, for drizzling
about 1–1.5 kg (2 lb 4 oz–3 lb 5 oz/
   4–6 cups) vegetable stock
250 g (9 oz) potatoes
5 g (¼ oz) flat-leaf parsley
salt and freshly ground black pepper

TO SERVE
toasted walnuts

Preheat your oven to 180°C fan (400°F/ gas 6). Slice the onion, leek and fennel and place on a baking tray (pan). Pick the thyme leaves and add along with the stripped stalks. Season with salt and pepper and drizzle with olive oil and mix to combine. Roast for 20–30 minutes, or until the veg are soft and beginning to colour.

Meanwhile, bring the stock to the boil in a large saucepan. Chop the potatoes, add to the boiling stock and cook until softened. When cooked, add the roasted veg (remove the thyme stalks) and parsley, then blitz (in a food processor or with a stick blender) until smooth, adding more stock if required. Season and serve with toasted walnuts and fennel fronds.

PEA AND COURGETTE

Serves 4–6

1 medium white onion
150 g (5 oz) potatoes
a drizzle of olive oil
1 courgette (zucchini)
300 g (10½ oz/2 cups) peas, fresh
   or frozen
50 g (2 oz) spinach
10 mint leaves
1 kg (2 lb 4 oz/4 cups) vegetable stock
juice of ½ small lemon
salt and freshly ground black pepper

TO SERVE
pea shoots
crème fraîche
grated Parmesan

Finely slice the onion and grate the potatoes coarsely.

Heat a little oil in a large saucepan over a medium heat, add the onion and potatoes and cook until softened. Grate the courgette and add to the pan along with the peas, spinach and mint leaves. Cover with the stock and bring to the boil. Cook for a few minutes before adding the lemon juice and a little seasoning.

Blitz (in a food processor or with a stick blender) until smooth, then season once more to taste.

Serve with some pea shoots, a dollop of crème fraîche, a generous grating of Parmesan and some black pepper.

CELERIAC AND APPLE

Serves 4–6

2 banana shallots
1 celery stalk
a drizzle of olive oil
2 apples
½ large celeriac (celery root), peeled
1–1.5 kg (2 lb 4 oz–3 lb 5 oz/4–6 cups)
   vegetable stock
2 sage leaves
salt and freshly ground black pepper

TO SERVE
fried sage leaves
toasted almonds
plain yoghurt
a drizzle of olive oil

Finely slice the shallots and celery.

Heat a little oil in a large saucepan over a medium heat, add the shallots and celery and cook until softened. Grate the apples and celeriac and add to the pan. Cover with 1 kg (2 lb 4 oz/4 cups) of the stock and add the sage leaves. Cover with a lid and cook for 20 minutes, or until everything is completely softened. You can top up with more stock if required.

Blitz (in a food processor or with a stick blender) until smooth and season to taste.

Serve with some crispy sage leaves, some toasted almonds, a drizzle of yoghurt and a drizzle of olive oil.

Ginger Noodles *with* Chilli Oil *and* Crumb

Serves 2

10 g (½ oz) dried whole
  Sichuan chillies
1 star anise
1 bay leaf
1 clove
1 tsp coriander seeds
1 tbsp sesame seeds
300 g (10½ oz/1¼ cups)
  peanut oil, plus extra for
  frying
150 g (5 oz) noodles
50 g (2 oz/¾ cup) panko
  breadcrumbs
10 g (½ oz) fresh ginger, cut
  into matchsticks
2 garlic cloves, finely
  chopped
½ tsp paprika
2 tsps soy sauce
2 tsps lime juice
1 spring onion (scallion),
  finely sliced
5 g (¼ oz) coriander
  (cilantro), finely chopped

SUBS
Sichuan chillies: dried
  chillies

Quick and fiery, and best scoffed at the same speed you made them! Any extra chilli oil can be kept in the refrigerator to be enjoyed with another batch of noodles or on top of a crispy fried egg later in the week.

Toast the chillies in a dry pan before blitzing them in a food processor until they look like flakes. Place them in a heatproof glass jar placed in a metal bowl (just in case the glass cracks with the heat – it has happened to me once and the clean-up was so messy so I am always extra cautious now!). Add the spices and sesame seeds.

Heat the peanut oil in a saucepan over a medium heat until it reaches 175°C/347°F. Very carefully pour it into the chilli jar (it will spit and sizzle). Set aside.

Cook your noodles according to the packet instructions.

Meanwhile, over a medium-high heat add a few more tbsps of peanut oil in the saucepan. When hot, add the breadcrumbs, half of the ginger and all of the garlic along with the paprika. Cook for a few minutes until golden brown and crispy. Set aside.

When ready to serve, spoon 1–2 tsps of the chilli oil into each serving bowl, then add a tsp of soy sauce and a tsp of lime juice to each. Divide the spring onion and coriander between the two bowls, then whisk everything together. Add the hot noodles and toss together. Finish with a sprinkling of crispy breadcrumbs, the remaining ginger and add more chilli oil, to taste.

The remaining chilli oil will keep in the sealed jar in the refrigerator for up to 1 month.

Grilled Mackerel *with* Parsley Salsa

Serves 2

30 g (1 oz) flat-leaf parsley

3 tbsps extra virgin olive oil

1 tbsp capers

1 garlic clove

juice of ½ lemon

250 g (9 oz) mixed cherry
    tomatoes

2 mackerel, butterflied

olive oil, for drizzling

fennel fronds and flowers
    (optional)

salt and freshly ground
    black pepper

SUBS

parsley – half basil and
    half dill

capers – 3 anchovies

mackerel – sardines

fennel fronds – dill

This is a perfectly light supper for a warm evening. It can be paired with lots of bread and colourful, jewel-like salads for a hungry household, but can also make for an excellent solo dinner with some potatoes and a few salad leaves.

Preheat the grill (broiler) to its highest setting.

In a food processor or using a stick blender and bowl, blitz together the parsley, oil, capers, garlic and lemon juice until very smooth. This should take roughly 2 minutes.

Chop the cherry tomatoes into small pieces – I like to do quarters or eighths, but this is entirely dependent on your patience!

Mix the parsley sauce with the tomatoes to create a vibrant green salsa. Season to taste and set aside.

Pat the mackerel fillets dry with kitchen paper to help the fish crisp up under the grill. Place on a roasting tray (pan), skin-side up, with a small piece of baking paper underneath (this helps prevent the fish from sticking to the tray, however you don't need too much as any excess may burn underneath the grill). Drizzle the skin with a little olive oil and season generously with some salt and pepper. Grill (broil) for 4–6 minutes depending on the size of your fish. The skin should blister and blacken a little and the flesh should be just cooked and flaking nicely.

Serve immediately with the salsa and some fennel fronds and flowers (or any other herbs you have to hand). This recipe is also delicious served with a dry white wine, but then again so is everything …

STORE CUPBOARD ESSENTIALS

CUPBOARD

Aleppo pepper or chilli (hot pepper)
   flakes

Almonds

Black pepper

Eggs

Garlic

Ginger

Hazelnuts

Light brown sugar

Olive oil and extra virgin olive oil

Pasta

Plain (all-purpose) flour

Salt

Shallots

Stock cubes

REFRIGERATOR & FREEZER

Butter

Cheese: ricotta, feta, mascarpone,
   Parmesan

Chocolate (good quality) (chocolate
   enjoyed from the refrigerator is an
   extra-special treat or midnight snack)

Chorizo or 'nduja (any charcuterie
   with a good shelf life)

Frozen broad (fava) beans and peas

Frozen sliced bread

Lemon

Parsley

Potatoes

Tomato purée

Wine (dry white)

TINNED & JARRED

Anchovies

Butter (lima) beans

Chickpeas (garbanzo beans)

Coconut milk

Gordal olives

Honey

Mustard

Roasted red (bell) peppers

SIMPLE SUPPERS FOR WHEN YOUR
CUPBOARDS ARE BARE

HAZELNUT AND SAGE PASTA

Serves 2
10 minutes

150 g (5 oz) trofie or farfalle or any pasta shape you have
50 g (2 oz) butter
5–7 sage leaves, finely chopped
1 garlic clove, finely sliced
50 g (2 oz/⅓ cup) roasted hazelnuts, roughly chopped
salt and freshly ground black pepper
grated Parmesan, to serve

SUBS
sage – rosemary; thyme; dried sage; dried thyme
hazelnuts – almonds; walnuts; pine nuts

Boil your pasta in salted water. Drain when cooked, reserving a little cooking water.

Meanwhile, heat the butter in a shallow frying pan (skillet) with some seasoning over a medium heat until beginning to foam. Add the sage, garlic and hazelnuts and cook for a few minutes, or until the garlic has softened and it is beginning to colour. Add a ladleful of the pasta cooking water into the sauce, then add the cooked pasta. Toss together and season to taste.

Serve with grated Parmesan.

ANCHOVY AND LEMON PASTA

Serves 2
10 minutes

150 g (5 oz) linguine or any pasta shape you have
a drizzle of olive oil
5–6 anchovy fillets
2 garlic cloves, finely sliced
1 tbsp capers
¼–½ tsp chilli (hot pepper) flakes
½ glass of white wine
10 g (½ oz) flat-leaf parsley, finely chopped
zest and juice of ½ lemon
salt and freshly ground black pepper

SUBS
anchovies – sardines
parsley – mint; rocket (arugula)

Boil your pasta in salted water. Drain when cooked, reserving a little cooking water.

Meanwhile, heat the olive oil in a shallow frying pan (skillet) over a medium heat. Add the anchovies, garlic, capers and chilli flakes and cook until the garlic has softened and coloured and the anchovies have almost melted into the oil. Add the wine and some seasoning and cook for a few minutes. Add a ladleful of the pasta water, along with the parsley and the lemon juice. Add the cooked pasta and toss together. Add a little more pasta water if required. Serve with the lemon zest.

LEMONY PEAS ON TOAST

Serves 2
10 minutes

150 g (7 oz/1¼ cups) frozen peas
5 g (¼ oz) flat-leaf parsley
5 g (¼ oz) mint
1 lemon
20 g (¾ oz) Parmesan
2 slices of sourdough
½ tsp Aleppo pepper
2 tbsps extra virgin olive oil
1 garlic clove, peeled
salt and freshly ground black pepper

Place the peas in a heatproof bowl and pour over boiling water. Allow to sit for 5 minutes.

Meanwhile, finely chop the herbs, zest half of the lemon and juice the whole lemon. Finely grate the Parmesan, then toast your bread.

Drain the peas, then use a fork to mash roughly. Add the herbs, lemon zest and juice, Parmesan, Aleppo pepper and oil. Season to taste.

Rub the toasted bread with the garlic before spooning over the pea mixture. This is nice finished with some more herbs and Parmesan, or maybe a crumble of feta if you have it.

OLIVE OIL FRITTATA

Serves 2
25 minutes

100 g (3½ oz/scant ½ cup) olive oil
1 large banana shallot, finely chopped
400 g (14 oz) potatoes, cut into 1 cm (½ in) cubes
4 eggs
salt and freshly ground black pepper

Heat the oil in a small non-stick frying pan (skillet), ideally with a lid, over a medium heat. Add the shallot and potatoes, turn the heat down to low and cover. Cook the potatoes for approx. 15 minutes, until they are completely soft.

In a bowl, whisk the eggs together with some seasoning. When the potatoes and onions are cooked, use a slotted spoon to remove them and add them to the bowl with the eggs. Mix well to combine. Keep any excess oil in the pan and place back over a medium-high heat. Add the egg mixture to the pan and stir gently with a spatula until the eggs set a little. Stop stirring and allow to cook for 2 minutes.

Run your spatula around the pan to loosen the frittata, then shake the pan gently to loosen it fully. Place a plate on top and flip quickly. Lift the frying pan off and return it to the heat. Add a little oil to the pan, then return the frittata to the pan, cooked-side up, for a further 3–4 minutes over a medium heat, or until cooked. Allow to sit for 5 minutes before serving.

SUPPER

TURKISH EGGS

Serves 2
10 minutes

175 g (6 oz/¾ cup) plain yoghurt
50 g (2 oz) butter
2 small garlic cloves
1 tsp Aleppo pepper
1 tbsp extra virgin olive oil
2 eggs
2 slices of sourdough
5 g (¼ oz) dill

salt and freshly ground black pepper

Mix the yoghurt with some seasoning and divide between 2 shallow bowls. Set aside to allow it to warm up a little.

Melt the butter in a small saucepan over a medium-high heat until beginning to brown. You don't want to burn it, but you are looking for a golden nutty colour. Meanwhile, finely chop one garlic clove. Remove the pan from the heat and add the garlic, Aleppo pepper and olive oil. The butter should foam a little. Swirl the pan to mix and set aside but keep warm.

Boil your kettle and use it to fill a second small saucepan of water and set over a high heat. Poach your eggs using your preferred method (this is a contentious subject and there is no right way! I like to add my eggs while the water is boiling rapidly, then turn the heat right down, but others prefer to use vinegar or swirl the water to make a whirlpool. The main thing is to make them your way!). Drain the eggs on a piece of kitchen paper to remove any excess water.

Toast your bread. Once done, rub the toast with the second peeled garlic clove while still hot – this is optional but I love the garlicky kick it gives.

To serve, place an egg in each bowl on top of the yoghurt, then generously spoon over the melted butter. Season well before garnishing with the dill (you can chop the dill or pick the fronds for this). Serve immediately with the toast.

FALAFEL

Serves 2–4 as a snack
20 minutes hands-on time – 1 hour total time

250 g (9 oz/generous 2 cups) frozen
   broad (fava) beans
1 × 400 g (14 oz) tin chickpeas
   (garbanzo beans), drained
1 tsp ground coriander
1 tsp ground cumin
½ tsp ground cinnamon
½ tsp Aleppo pepper or chilli
   (hot pepper) flakes
½ tsp ground black pepper
1 tbsp tahini
15 g (¼ oz) fresh herbs (I like flat-leaf
   parsley, coriander/cilantro and mint)
2 garlic cloves, minced
4 spring onions (scallions),
   roughly chopped
1 tsp salt
½ tsp baking powder
sunflower oil, for deep-frying
sesame seeds, for rolling

TO SERVE
tahini sauce (tahini mixed with a little water,
   lemon juice, garlic, salt and pepper)
toasted pine nuts or almonds
plenty of fresh herbs

Place the frozen beans in a heatproof bowl and cover with boiling water. Set aside for 5 minutes or until cool enough to handle. Squeeze the beans out of their shells and discard the shells.

Blitz the drained chickpeas and the shelled beans in a food processor until smooth. Add 3 tbsps of water, all the spices, tahini and herbs and blitz again. Add the garlic, spring onions, salt and baking powder and blitz until smooth.

Heat a little oil in a frying pan (skillet) and cook a small amount of the mixture to check for seasoning. Adjust accordingly.

Place the falafel mix in the refrigerator, covered, for 30 minutes.

Fill a large saucepan a quarter full of oil and heat over a high heat. When the oil reaches 180°C/350°F, turn the heat down a little and begin cooking.

Fill a saucer with sesame seeds. Remove the falafel mix from the refrigerator and use 2 spoons dipped in boiling water to shape the falafel mixture into ovals. Roll each one in the seeds before lowering into the hot oil. Fry for a few minutes on each side until golden brown in batches of 4–5. Remove with a slotted spoon to drain on some kitchen paper.

Serve warm with some tahini sauce, some toasted pine nuts or almonds, and plenty of fresh herbs.

WELSH RAREBIT

Serves 2
10 minutes

25 g (¾ oz) butter, plus extra to butter
    the toast
100 g (3½ oz/scant ½ cup) stout or ale
    (milk will also work if you don't have
    any in the house, but you may need
    a bit more seasoning)
1 tsp plain (all-purpose) flour
1 tsp Dijon mustard
1 tsp grainy mustard
1 tsp Worcestershire sauce, plus more
    to serve
175 g (6 oz) strong Cheddar, grated
2 slices of sourdough, toasted
salt and freshly ground black pepper

Heat the grill (broiler) to high.

Melt the butter in a small pan with the
stout and flour. Whisk to combine and
cook over a medium heat until thickened
slightly. Add the mustards and the
Worcestershire sauce to the pan, then add
the Cheddar. Continue to cook over a
medium–low heat, making sure it doesn't
boil, until just melted. Season to taste.

Butter your toast, then spoon over the
cheesy mixture. Grill (broil) for a few
minutes until beginning to colour and
blister.

Splash more Worcestershire sauce on
the top and eat immediately.

ROASTED TOMATO SOUP

Serves 2–4
20 minutes hands-on time – 1 hour total time

2 × 400 g (14 oz) tins peeled plum tomatoes
2 small red onions
4 garlic cloves
1 tsp dried oregano
75 g (2½ oz) stale bread
olive oil, for drizzling
200 g (7 oz/scant 1 cup) vegetable stock
1–2 tsps white wine vinegar
salt and freshly ground black pepper

TO SERVE
grated Parmesan, basil leaves

Preheat the oven to 220°C fan (475°F/
gas 9). Drain the tomatoes, reserving
the liquid in a large saucepan. Cut the
tomatoes in half and arrange on a roasting
tray (pan). Peel then cut the onions into
eighths and add to the tray. Skin the garlic
cloves and add along with the oregano.
Roughly chop the stale bread and add
to the tray with a glug of oil and some
seasoning. Roast for 20–30 minutes or
until golden.

Transfer everything from the tray into the
saucepan with the reserved tomato juice.
Deglaze the tray with a little boiling water
and add to the pan with the stock and the
vinegar, then bring to a simmer. Blitz in a
food processor until smooth. Add more
stock if required. Season to taste and
serve with some grated Parmesan, basil
leaves and a little oil.

CHAPTER TWO

Thirty-minute *tea*

Roasted Ricotta, Broad Beans
and Courgette

Serves 2–4 as a side dish

500 g (1 lb 2 oz) courgettes
   (zucchini)
250 g (9 oz) ricotta, drained
8 garlic cloves, unpeeled
olive oil, for drizzling
a small bunch of thyme
a small bunch of fresh
   oregano
150 g (5 oz/1¼ cups) shelled
   broad (fava) beans
25 g (¾ oz) dill, finely
   chopped

TO SERVE
15 g (½ oz) mixture of flat-
   leaf parsley and chives,
   to finish
sourdough bread
salt and freshly ground
   black pepper

SUBS
ricotta – feta (this will be
   saltier, so season
   accordingly)
thyme – marjoram
broad (fava) beans – fresh
   peas

I enjoy this as a simple, light supper or side dish in summer when the courgettes are bountiful. You can bulk up the recipe by cooking 250 g (9 oz/2½ cups) of orzo in some stock. Drain and reserve a little of the liquid, then stir it through the courgette, ricotta and beans when cooked.

Preheat the oven to 200°C fan (430°F/gas 8).

Chop the courgette into rough discs. Place the ricotta in the middle of a deep roasting tray (pan) and surround it with the courgettes and the whole garlic cloves. Generously drizzle with some olive oil and season with some salt and pepper. Nestle the oregano and thyme stalks (leaving them whole) in among the courgettes. Bake for 20–30 minutes, or until the courgettes are golden and the ricotta has firmed up.

Meanwhile, pour some boiling water into a heatproof bowl and add the shelled broad beans. Leave to sit for 10 minutes or until the water has cooled down enough to handle. Gently squeeze out the beans from the shells – they should do this easily, but if they are more stubborn simply drain the water and repeat the process by adding more boiling water. Discard the shells and place the beans in a bowl.

Heat another glug of olive oil in a medium frying pan (skillet) over a high heat. Add the beans and cook for a few minutes, making sure you don't overcook them. You simply want to colour the skin a little, so hot and fast is the best method for this. Remove from the heat and add the dill. Stir through with a little seasoning.

Remove the roasting tray from the oven and use a fork or a knife to remove the herbs from their stalks (discard them).

When ready to serve, spoon the courgettes and garlic onto a platter. Gently break up the ricotta into rough pieces and scatter over the courgettes. Spoon over the fried beans, drizzle with any extra oil from both the roasting tray and the frying pan, and garnish with the herbs. Serve with toasted sourdough. This is delicious when you squeeze a couple of the garlic cloves out of their skin and spread over the toast before topping with the courgettes, ricotta and beans.

Cannellini Beans, Olive Sauce, Cavolo Nero *and* Aioli

Serves 4 or 6 as a side dish

150 g (5 oz) cavolo nero

1 banana shallot

2 garlic cloves

1 rosemary sprig

olive oil, for cooking

50 g (2 oz/3 tbsps) vermouth

2 × 400 g (14 oz) tins
   cannellini beans, drained

200 g (7 oz/scant 1 cup)
   vegetable stock

salt and freshly ground
   black pepper

grated salted ricotta or
   pecorino, to serve

FOR THE SAUCE

50 g (2 oz/scant ½ cup)
   green olives, pitted

1 tbsp capers

100 g (3½ oz/scant ½ cup)
   olive oil

1 garlic clove

10 g (½ oz) flat-leaf parsley

10 g (½ oz) basil

FOR THE AIOLI

1 egg

½ tsp Dijon mustard

1 garlic clove

100 g (3½ oz/scant ½ cup)
sunflower oil

100 g (3½ oz/scant ½ cup)
olive oil

1 tbsp lemon juice

salt and freshly ground
   black pepper

When making aioli or mayonnaise in these smaller quantities, I much prefer to use the whole egg to avoid waste. If you prefer a richer egg-yolk-yellow aioli and will use some white for meringues later, by all means use two yolks in place of the one egg. Equally, if you are short on time and don't want to see the egg white forgotten in the back of the refrigerator, a whole egg works perfectly well.

Remove the stalks from the cavolo nero and chop up finely. Cut the leaves into 2 cm (¾ in) chunks and set aside. Finely slice the shallot and garlic. Strip the rosemary leaves.

Heat a little oil in a large pan over a medium heat, add the chopped cavolo nero stalks, onion, garlic and rosemary, and sweat down until softened and beginning to colour. Add the vermouth and cook for 1–2 minutes, then add the drained cannellini beans and stock. Reduce the heat to low and cover with a lid.

To make the sauce, blitz together all the ingredients in a food processor until well combined and still quite coarse. Season to taste and set aside.

To make the aioli, put the egg, mustard, a little seasoning and the garlic into a food processor (I often use the same one used for the sauce without cleaning it, as it will add a little flavour to the aioli). Blitz, then with the motor still running, add the oils in a slow trickle, making sure the aioli doesn't split. If your aioli does split, add a tbsp of boiling water and mix again to try to re-emulsify. Sometimes, you might need to add a few tbsps, but make sure you don't add too many and allow a few minutes of mixing in between each

SUBS

cannellini beans – butter
   (lima) beans

vermouth – white wine

basil – chervil; coriander
   (cilantro)

cavolo nero – chard; kale

one. Once thick and when all the oil has been added, whisk in the lemon juice. Season again, to taste.

Add the reserved cavolo nero leaves to the pan with the beans and mix well. Cook for 1–2 minutes, adding more stock if required. Finally, stir in the olive sauce and season to taste.

Serve in bowls, with a generous dollop of the aioli on top and lots of grated salted ricotta or pecorino.

Fennel, Tomato *and* Sardine Toasts

Serves 4

olive oil, for drizzling
1 small fennel bulb, finely
   sliced lengthways
4 garlic cloves: 3 finely
   sliced; 1 peeled
¼ tsp fennel seeds
pinch of thyme (fresh or
   dried)
pinch of paprika
50 g (2 oz/3 tbsps) white
   wine
125 g (4 oz) heritage
   tomatoes, roughly sliced
50 g (2 oz/3 tbsps) extra
   virgin olive oil
zest and juice of ½ lemon
¼ tsp chilli (hot pepper)
   flakes
10 g (½ oz) flat-leaf parsley,
   finely chopped
4–6 fresh sardines
2 large slices of sourdough
salt and freshly ground
   black pepper

SUBS
fennel – 2–3 banana
   shallots
heritage tomatoes – cherry
   or plum tomatoes
parsley – dill

Things on toast is my default position when making dinner. This recipe was first made late one night to use up some forgotten fennel, but has since become a staple and is adapted regularly in order to use up bits and pieces.

Heat a drizzle of olive oil in a medium saucepan over a medium heat. Add the fennel and sweat until beginning to colour and soften, then add the garlic, fennel seeds, thyme and paprika. Cook until the finely sliced garlic has softened, then add the white wine and allow to simmer for a few minutes or until the alcohol has cooked off (it shouldn't smell boozy). Stir in the tomatoes and cook for no more than a minute. Set aside to infuse but keep warm.

In a bowl, whisk together the extra virgin olive oil, lemon zest and juice, chilli and parsley. Season to taste.

Heat a frying pan (skillet) over a high heat. Pat the sardines dry, drizzle with a little oil and season lightly with salt and pepper. Fry the sardines on both sides until slightly charred and cooked through (the time will depend on their size, but little ones should only take a minute or two). The aim is to cook them quickly. Remove from the pan to a plate and spoon over the oil and lemon mixture. Toast the sourdough in the pan while it is still hot.

To serve, rub the toasted sourdough slices with the fresh peeled garlic clove. Place on plates then spoon the warm fennel and tomatoes over the top. Top with the sardines and spoon over any extra oil.

Butter Beans, Artichoke
and Steak

Serves 2

drizzle of olive oil

150 g (5 oz) onions (I like
   to use a mix of spring
   onions/scallions, shallots
   and red onions), finely
   chopped to the same size
   pieces

4 garlic cloves, finely sliced

100 g (3½ oz/scant ½ cup)
   white wine

1 × 400 g (14 oz) tin butter
   (lima) beans, drained

285 g (10 oz) jar artichokes
   in oil, drained (reserve
   the artichoke oil
   for making mayonnaise
   or cooking with)

200-250 g (7 oz/¾ cups)
   good-quality vegetable
   or chicken stock

salt and freshly ground
   black pepper

FOR THE STEAK

200–300 g (7–10½ oz) steak
   (I often find the quality
   of the meat is more
   important than the cut –
   fillet is delicious if you
   are celebrating, but rump,
   sirloin or any of the other
   'cheaper' cuts can be
   equally as delicious when
   they come from a well-
   looked-after animal)

James would almost always pair steak with chips and peppercorn sauce. Although I do love that classic combo, I am secretly much more of a fan of this pairing.

If making the optional lovage oil, blanch the lovage leaves in some boiling water, then drain. Allow to cool for a minute, then squeeze out any excess water. Place in a pan with the olive oil and heat gently. You want to heat the oil to no higher than 75°C/167°F. Transfer to a food processor and blitz for 2–3 minutes, or until smooth and well combined. Strain through a muslin cloth, then set aside. I sometimes like to stir a tbspful of the leftover pulp from the cloth through the beans once they are cooked for an extra herby kick.

Heat a little olive oil in a large frying pan (skillet) over a medium heat. Add the onions and cook slowly until soft. Add the garlic and cook for a few more minutes until everything is soft and just starting to turn golden. Add the white wine and increase the heat to medium-high. Once the wine has reduced a little, add the butter beans and artichokes, and stir through until well coated. Add the stock, season a little, then reduce the heat. Simmer for 15 minutes, ensuring the beans and artichokes don't overcook.

Meanwhile, prepare the steaks. Allow them to come to room temperature for at least 10 minutes. Heat a medium cast-iron pan over a high heat until just smoking. Season the steaks lightly with some salt and pepper and place in the pan. Cook on either side for a few minutes, then continue to cook and flip every minute or so. Once the steaks have a good colour to them, I like to add the butter, thyme and garlic together and use the melted butter and the herbs to baste the steaks.

50 g (2 oz) butter

a few thyme sprigs

4 garlic cloves

salt and freshly ground
black pepper

FOR THE LOVAGE OIL
(optional)

25 g (¾ oz) lovage leaves
or flat-leaf parsley, plus
extra to garnish

75 g (2½ oz/5 tbsps) olive oil

SUBS

white wine – chicken or veg
stock

butter (lima) beans –
cannellini beans

thyme – rosemary

For this dish, I like my steak medium-rare, but this will depend on the cut, the size and the quality of meat. Look for an internal temperature of 60–70°C/140–158°F or use your fingers to gauge the doneness. Once cooked, set aside in a deep plate and pour the cooking juices, herbs and garlic onto the steaks. Cover and allow to rest for 5–10 minutes.

To serve, spoon the hot bean mixture into shallow bowls, slice the steak and place carefully over the top and spoon over any resting juices. Finish with a drizzle of the lovage oil (if using), then add some parsley and young lovage leaves, if desired.

A SIMPLE SAUCE AND
ITS MANY USES

BÉCHAMEL SAUCE

700 g (1 lb 9 oz/scant 3 cups) whole (full-fat) milk
1 bay leaf
1 thyme sprig, leaves finely chopped
1 rosemary sprig, leaves finely chopped
70 g (2½ oz) butter
50 g (2 oz/scant ½ cup) plain (all-purpose) flour
nutmeg for grating
50 g (2 oz) Parmesan, grated
50 g (2 oz) Cheddar, grated
salt and freshly ground black pepper

Optional additions
1 small white onion, quartered
2 garlic cloves, unpeeled but squashed

If you have time, I recommend infusing the milk. Heat the milk with the bay leaf, thyme, rosemary, and optional onion and garlic, in a large saucepan. Once simmering, remove from the heat and let it infuse for 30 minutes. Strain the milk.

In a large saucepan, melt the butter with the flour over a medium heat. Add the milk in 4 stages, whisking well and allowing the mixture to thicken in between. Whisk out all lumps before adding more milk. If you haven't infused the milk, add the bay leaf, thyme and rosemary during the first addition. Keep adding the milk until it is used up and your sauce is glossy. Season well and add a grating of nutmeg. Stir in the cheeses and season. Cover and set aside. Remove the bay leaf before using.

CROQUE MONSIEUR

Serves 4

½ quantity of Béchamel Sauce (left)
4 large croissants or 8 slices of
    sourdough or white bread
50 g (¾ oz) butter, melted
Dijon mustard
good-quality sliced ham
100 g (3½ oz) Gruyère cheese, grated
100 g (3½ oz) Comté cheese, grated
freshly ground black pepper
cornichons, to serve

Prepare the béchamel as instructed on the left, then set aside to cool down.

Preheat the oven to 200°C fan (430°F/ gas 8). If using croissants, cut them in half. Arrange the croissants or slices of bread on a baking tray (pan) and brush with the melted butter. Place in the oven for 2–3 minutes.

Spread Dijon mustard on one half of each sandwich, then top each with the ham and a generous amount of the béchamel. Add a third of each cheese to each sandwich. Season with black pepper, then top with the other halves of the sandwiches. Pour the last of the béchamel over the top, then sprinkle over the last of the cheeses. Place in the oven for 10 minutes, or until golden. Serve with the cornichons on the side.

CHESTNUT AND BACON RIGATONI PASTA

Serves 4–6

1 quantity of Béchamel Sauce (opposite)
300 g (10½ oz) rigatoni or penne pasta
200 g (7 oz) smoked streaky bacon
100 g (3½ oz) cooked chestnuts
a drizzle of olive oil
5 g (¼ oz) sage leaves, finely chopped
2 thyme sprigs, leaves picked
10 g (½ oz) flat-leaf parsley,
   finely chopped
50 g (2 oz) pecorino or Parmesan
salt and freshly ground black pepper

Prepare the béchamel as instructed opposite.

Bring a large saucepan of salted water to the boil, add the pasta and cook for 8–10 minutes, or until al dente. Drain, reserving a little of the cooking water.

Meanwhile, chop the bacon and chestnuts into roughly 5 mm (¼ in) chunks.

Heat a little olive oil in a large frying pan (skillet) over a medium heat. Add the bacon and allow to crisp up a little before stirring in the chestnuts. After a few minutes, add the sage and thyme. Once everything is crispy and golden, remove from the heat. Use a slotted spoon to remove the bacon and chestnuts and set aside.

Add the béchamel to the pan with a little of the pasta water. Add the cooked pasta and toss together to combine. Stir in the parsley.

Divide among plates, then top with the crispy bacon and chestnuts. Grate over the cheese and add a generous crack of black pepper, serve immediately.

CAVOLO NERO, SAUSAGE AND RICOTTA LASAGNE

Serves 6

1 quantity of Béchamel Sauce (pg. 60)
500 g (1 lb 2 oz/2 cups) milk
200 g (7 oz) cavolo nero
olive oil, for drizzling
350 g (12 oz) leeks or red onions,
  finely sliced
4 garlic cloves, finely sliced
400 g (14 oz) sausages
butter, for greasing
300–350 g (12 oz) dried lasagne sheets
250 g (9 oz) ricotta
75 g (2½ oz) your preferred cheese
  for topping
freshly ground black pepper
thyme leaves, to garnish

Preheat the oven to 180°C fan (400°F/ gas 6).

Prepare the béchamel as instructed on page 60. Once ready, whisk in the additional milk (you can add a wee splash of cream if you are looking for something extra-silky). This extra liquid is necessary when using dried pasta sheets, as they absorb much more moisture than you expect. Although the béchamel will feel quite thin, it will thicken up when baking.

Remove the stalks from the cavolo nero and finely chop them, then cut the leaves into rough pieces. Heat the oil in a large frying pan (skillet) over a medium heat. Add the sliced cavolo nero stalks along with the leeks and cook until softened and beginning to colour. Add the garlic and cook for a few minutes, then add the chopped cavolo nero leaves and cook until softened. Remove the greens from the pan and set aside in a bowl.

Place the pan back on the heat. Remove the sausage meat from its casings and add to the pan. Use a wooden spoon to break the meat up into smaller pieces. Cook for 5 minutes over a high heat or until well coloured all over.

To assemble, grease a 20 × 30 cm (8 × 12 in) baking tin (pan). Pour a fifth of the béchamel into the base and top with 4 lasagne sheets. Spoon over a third of the greens, then a third of the sausagemeat, then another fifth of the béchamel and lastly a third of the ricotta. Add a further 4 sheets of lasagne, then repeat this process until the fillings are all used up (you should have a fifth of the béchamel left over for the topping). Finish with a final 4 sheets of lasagne, then spoon over the last of the béchamel. Grate your favourite cheese over the top, then grind over some black pepper, add a little drizzle of oil and a sprinkle of thyme leaves.

Bake for 40–45 minutes, or until the pasta is cooked through and soft when a knife is inserted into the middle.

SUPPER

Charred Corn Dal

Serves 4

olive oil, for cooking
2 whole corn on the cob
2 banana shallots, finely
  sliced
4 garlic cloves, finely sliced
about 10 g (½ oz) fresh
  ginger, finely sliced
1 small red chilli (remove
  seeds for less spice)
1 tsp ground turmeric
1 tsp ground coriander
1 tsp nigella seeds, plus
  extra to garnish
½ tsp cumin seeds
½ tsp mustard seeds
150 g (5 oz/scant ⅔ cup)
  red lentils
1 × 400 g (14 oz) tin coconut
  milk
200 g (7 oz/scant 1 cup)
  vegetable stock
100 g (3½ oz) cherry
  tomatoes
juice of ½ lemon
10 g (½ oz) coriander
  (cilantro), stalks and
  leaves separated
100 g (3½ oz/generous
  ⅓ cup) yoghurt
juice of 1 lime
salt and freshly ground
  black pepper

I love dals for their satisfying and warming properties, but equally for their versatility. This would be delicious served as is or with some warmed garlicky flatbreads as part of a fragrant feast.

Heat a heavy-based griddle pan over a high heat. Add a little oil, and when nearly smoking add the whole sweetcorn. Turn the sweetcorn frequently until they have a good char on the outside. This works even better if done over a barbecue. If cooking over fire you can make the dal over the flame too, just make sure you let it die down a little. Once the sweetcorn is charred, set aside.

Heat a little olive oil in a heavy-based saucepan over a medium heat. Add the shallots and cook for 5 minutes until golden brown and softened. Add the garlic and ginger and cook for a further few minutes. Add all the spices and cook for another couple of minutes until toasted. Add the lentils, coconut milk and stock. Chop the tomatoes in half, then add to the pan too. Season well, cover and cook for 20–30 minutes until the lentils have softened, stirring frequently.

Slice the corn off the cobs and stir into the dal with the lemon juice. Season to taste. You may need to add a little more veg stock to thin, if required.

Finely chop the coriander stalks and stir into the yoghurt along with the lime juice. Season to taste.

When ready to eat, pour the dal into bowls and spoon over the yoghurt mixture. Garnish with the coriander leaves and some more nigella seeds.

Barley Risotto

Serves 2 (with a little extra
left over for some
Arancini, page 207)

olive oil, for cooking

70 g (2½ oz) spring onions
(scallions), finely chopped

2 celery stalks, finely
chopped

3 garlic cloves, finely sliced

200 g (7 oz/scant 1 cup)
pearl barley

100 g (3½ oz/scant ½ cup)
white wine

1 Parmesan rind

1–1.25 kg (2 lb 4 oz–2 lb 13 oz/
4–5 cups) chicken stock

50 g (2 oz) butter

50 g (2 oz) salty cheese
(ideally Parmesan or
Grana Padano, but I have
used mature Cheddar for
this recipe before and
it wasn't terrible!), finely
grated, plus extra to serve

juice of ½ lemon

20 g (¾ oz) flat-leaf parsley,
finely chopped

salt and freshly ground
black pepper

SUBS

spring onions – red onions
or shallots

celery – can be omitted or
use about 75 g (2½ oz)
finely chopped leek

Barley always makes me think of warming soups and broths, but it can be equally as delicious here. It brings a lovely nuttiness to the risotto that would pair nicely with some crispy sage or roasted squash. This also makes for some great arancini, so it is worth showing some restraint with portion sizes (or simply make double!).

Heat a little olive oil in a large frying pan (skillet) over a medium heat, add the onions and celery and sweat until softened. Add the garlic and stir to combine. Add the pearl barley and cook for a few minutes until toasted and beginning to colour on the edges. Pour in the wine and add the Parmesan rind. Stir to mix through, then begin adding the stock gradually, a ladleful at a time. Make sure you stir the risotto well in between additions. Season lightly at this stage. Continue this process for 20–30 minutes, or until the barley has absorbed most of the liquid but still has a little bite to it.

Remove from the heat and add the butter and cheese. Beat well until the butter and cheese have completely melted and created a glossy sauce. Stir in the lemon juice, then stir in the parsley. Season once more, to taste.

Serve immediately with a little more grated cheese on top. Use any leftover risotto to make the Arancini on page 207.

You can add any additions you like to this risotto, but some of my favourites are:

– leftover roast chicken (mix in the last 5–10 minutes of stock additions) – if you have roasted onions and garlic from your chicken, add these in too

pearl barley – arborio rice (liquid quantities will need to be adjusted a little)

white wine – 1 tbsp white vinegar and the rest of the weight made up with whatever stock you are using

parsley – dill

– wild garlic

– peas – a mixture of sliced sugar snap and shelled garden peas is lovely (add in the last few minutes of cooking)

– roasted leeks

– cooked and grated beetroot (beets) makes for a vibrant risotto – serve with crumbled goat's cheese

EATING ALONE AND
OTHER SIMPLE PLEASURES

I have spoken a lot about the fact that this book is designed to encourage you to cook for those you live with or spend most days in the company of. However, I wanted to add a note for those who don't have a housemate or partner, or happen to spend most of their meals eating alone. When the media or books discuss the topic of mealtimes (mainly dinner), images with groups of people often accompany and perhaps alienate those who eat solo most nights. It seems a shame to me, as many meals I have eaten have been alone and joyous in their own way.

As a student I ate alone almost exclusively and it allowed me an opportunity to experiment with both my taste, cooking ability and appetite for trying something new. As I mention, cooking for your household can be almost freeing when you realise that there tends to be very little expectation for perfection, and the same applies when cooking for yourself. It's hugely liberating to be able to cater entirely for your own preferences, and without the worry of what other people do or do not enjoy.

As a cook and caterer, it is almost impossible not to care about what other people like or dislike, and as a perfectionist it can be crippling. I spend a huge amount of time apologising for my own tastes or how I indulge in one thing or another. And don't even get me started on when I am cooking for other cooks … I personally find it to be a great pleasure to consider only what I do or don't want to eat that night. Particularly in this day and age, when we have to consider other people's wants and needs so frequently it can become exhausting.

There is also a lot to be said about appreciating the value of food when eating solo. If you have bought and spent money on a particularly special cheese, vegetable or loaf, you will gain far more pleasure from eating it alone and knowing its source and cost than watching others tear into it greedily and without thought. It's a simple pleasure to shop and eat for yourself.

I love to take time when cooking for myself and only recently have I realised that I can gain as much pleasure from setting the table for one as I would for a feast. A candlelight supper for one is a simple pleasure I often only experience in restaurants. In my opinion, it can be just as enjoyable to do at home. I spoke about the stress-relieving properties that come from feeding those in your house, but the same applies when feeding yourself. You may consume enough pasta to feed a small army without so much as a raised eyebrow from another soul. What's not to love about that?

Please cook and indulge in these recipes solo, regardless of how many people you do or don't have under your roof, and please take the time and effort to indulge yourself. No one has to know you secretly hate oysters (me) or enjoy a snack consisting solely of multiple spoonfuls of extra-thick double cream (also me). It is entirely up to you – and, frankly, you deserve it.

SCALLOPS IN THEIR SHELLS

softened butter (10–15 g/½ oz per scallop)

flat-leaf parsley

garlic

chilli (hot pepper) flakes

baby capers

fennel fronds

scallops (however many you want
   to eat), still in their shell

lemon

salt and freshly ground black pepper

Preheat the grill (broiler) to its highest setting.

Place the softened butter in a bowl. Finely chop some parsley and add to the butter along with some seasoning. Mince a little garlic and add to the bowl along with a small pinch of chilli flakes, if using (be very sparing here, as you don't want to overpower the beautiful scallop flesh). Finely chop some baby capers and fennel fronds, then mix in for a lovely green butter.

Spoon the butter over the scallop shells and place on a baking tray (pan). Place under the grill for a few minutes (this will depend on their size), or until they are just cooked through. The butter will help keep the scallops soft.

Once cooked, squeeze over a little lemon juice and eat immediately. A nice baguette makes for a good partner here, to help mop up any escaped butter.

CHEDDAR AND KIMCHI TOASTIE

2 slices of sourdough

mayo

50 g (2 oz) good-quality Cheddar
   (I use St Andrews Cheddar)

25 g (¾ oz) Gruyère (or another cheese
   of your choosing)

35 g (1¼ oz) kimchi

5 g (¼ oz) coriander (cilantro) leaves

butter

cornichons, to serve

Spread both slices of the bread with mayo. Grate both of the cheeses. Spread the kimchi onto one side of the sandwich, then top with the grated cheese. Finely chop the coriander and sprinkle over the top. Place the second piece of bread on top.

Spread the outside of the sandwich with butter and fry for a few minutes on each side in a frying pan (skillet) over a medium heat until golden and crisp and oozing in the middle.

Serve with cornichons.

A SIMPLE CHICKEN PIE

1 small banana shallot or 2 spring
    onions (scallions)
a drizzle of olive oil
1 tbsp plain (all-purpose) flour
25 g (¾ oz) butter
50 g (2 oz/3 tbsps) white wine or cider
    (depending on what you want
    to drink with it)
100 g (3½ oz/scant ½ cup) chicken stock
½ tsp grainy mustard
2 tbsps crème fraîche
1 small rosemary sprig
1 small tarragon or thyme sprig
about 100 g (3½ oz) leftover roast chicken,
    picked from the carcass
a few sheets of filo pastry
melted butter, for brushing
thyme leaves
salt and freshly ground black pepper

Preheat the oven to 200°C fan (430°F/ gas 8).

Finely slice the shallot lengthways, then add to a saucepan with a little oil and cook over a medium heat until golden brown. Add the flour and butter and cook for another few moments. Pour in the wine or cider and cook until the booze has cooked off (it shouldn't smell overly alcoholic). Add the stock and the mustard and crème fraîche, then the herbs and the chicken. Cook for about 5 minutes, adding a little more stock if required, until thickened and flavoursome. Season to taste.

Pour into a small ovenproof dish or a wee pie dish. Scrunch up some filo pastry and place on top. Brush generously with melted butter and sprinkle with some thyme leaves. Bake for 15–20 minutes, or until golden brown (make sure the filo doesn't burn).

Serve immediately.

ASPARAGUS OMELETTE

50 g (2 oz) asparagus spears

2 eggs

10 g (½ oz) finely grated pecorino,
    plus extra to serve

10 g (½ oz) mixed herbs (dill, fennel,
    coriander/cilantro and chives will all work),
    finely chopped

olive oil, for cooking

1 spring onion (scallion), finely chopped

5 g (¼ oz) flat-leaf parsley, finely chopped

30 g (1 oz) Brie

zest of ¼ lemon

salt and freshly ground black pepper

finely chopped dill fronds, to serve

Preheat the grill (broiler) to its highest setting.

Dry fry the asparagus spears in a small non-stick frying pan (skillet) until golden (you shouldn't need any oil as you are just aiming to get some colour on them). Remove from the pan and set aside.

Whisk the eggs together in a bowl with a generous amount of seasoning. Mix in the pecorino and mixed herbs.

Heat a little oil in the same pan over a medium-high heat. Pour in the eggs and cook untouched for 20–30 seconds, then use a rubber spatula to gently pull the edges of the omelette into the centre. This should create soft folds in the egg and allow the uncooked egg to flood the gaps left behind. Leave to cook again for a few more seconds, then repeat the process. When just about set, arrange the asparagus over one half of the omelette. Scatter over the spring onion and parsley, then crumble the Brie on top. Fold the omelette in half and garnish with the lemon zest.

Serve immediately with some more grated pecorino and the dill fronds.

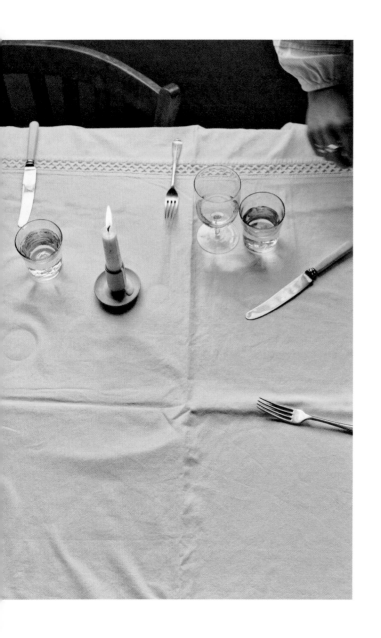

CHAPTER THREE

Good things to drink (and eat!)

Vodka Fizz

Serves 2

ice

60 g (2¼ oz/¼ cup) vodka

20 g (3¼ oz/1½ tbsps)
lemon juice (pare 2 strips
of the lemon zest before
juicing to give you your
twists for garnishing)

20 g (3¼ oz/1½ tbsps)
apple juice

20 g (3¼ oz/1½ tbsps)
simple syrup (1 part sugar
to 1 part water, brought to
the boil until the sugar
dissolves. Allow to cool
before using)

6 large sage leaves

prosecco, to top up

SUBS

lemon juice – lime juice

simple syrup – elderflower
cordial

prosecco – Crémant or soda
water

This is based on a cocktail called the Fizzy Rascal by Oskar Kinberg, who wrote the brilliant (and much-used in our house) *Cocktail Cookbook*. It has caused many a sore head since I started making them. I have adapted it slightly, so this version is a little weaker (60 g/2¼ oz for two instead of the heady 50 g/2 oz for one in the original version) and I don't like to use elderflower liqueur.

Fill a cocktail shaker with ice, then add the vodka, lemon juice, apple juice and simple syrup as well as 4 of the sage leaves. Shake vigorously for 1 minute, then strain into 2 highball glasses filled with ice. Top up with prosecco, then garnish with the remaining sage leaves and a twist of lemon each.

Basil Gimlet

*Makes enough syrup for
8 cocktails*

FOR THE SYRUP
100 g (3½ oz/scant ½ cup)
   caster (superfine) sugar
100 g (3½ oz/scant ½ cup)
   water
35 g (1¼ oz) basil (stalks
   and all)
50 g (2 oz/3 tbsps) lime juice
   (from about 5 limes)

TO SERVE
gin
ice
basil leaves

SUBS
caster sugar – demerara
   (for a more complex
   sweetness)
basil – you can transform
   this into any type of
   gimlet really by using
   different herbs – mint
   works best and you can
   swap the basil out for an
   equal weight; tarragon is
   also good, but you will
   need a considerable
   amount less, as it is such
   a punchy herb – add a
   little at a time to taste

For Granny Joan, who loves this recipe.

Bring the sugar and the water to the boil in a pan until all the sugar has dissolved, then set aside to cool.

Add the cooled syrup to a food processor along with the basil and lime juice. Blitz for 3–4 minutes or until smooth and well combined. Strain through a muslin cloth for a clearer cocktail or simply a sieve if you aren't as fussy!

To serve, shake 1 part basil mix to 1 part gin in an ice-filled cocktail shaker. Strain into a small coupe glass or similar and garnish with a basil leaf. For a weaker drink, pour over ice.

The basil mixture will keep in the refrigerator for up to 3 days (you may notice it discolours slightly, but this is fine).

Fennel *and* Ginger

Serves 4

FOR THE SYRUP

1 tbsp fennel seeds

150 g (5 oz/⅔ cup) caster
   (superfine) sugar

150 g (5 oz/⅔ cup) water

TO SERVE

5 g (¼ oz) mint leaves

1 tsp fennel seeds

ice

100 g (3½ oz/scant ½ cup)
   gin

50 g (2 oz/3 tbsps) lime juice

cold ginger beer (choose
   one that isn't too sweet),
   to top up

fennel flowers and fronds,
   to garnish

SUBS

caster sugar – demerara

gin – vodka

Not a million miles away from the Moscow Mule (although I use gin here), this recipe has a subtle and refreshing flavour from the addition of fennel. The fennel syrup lasts well in the refrigerator and has many different uses. You can, of course, make more cocktails, mix it into fruit salads, or simply add a splash into a glass of prosecco for a less punchy drink. This is also great if used with cakes. Simply brush over a still-warm sponge (lemon is best). It will help moisten and sweeten the cake.

To make the syrup, bash the fennel seeds in a pestle and mortar, then place in a pan with the sugar and water. Bring to the boil and simmer for 5 minutes, then remove from the heat and set aside to infuse for 30 minutes. Strain into a glass jar and store in the refrigerator for up to 1 month until ready to serve.

To make the cocktails, bash together the mint and the fennel seeds in a pestle and mortar. Add to a cocktail shaker and fill with ice. Pour in the gin, lime juice and 100 g (3½ oz/scant ½ cup) of the fennel syrup. Shake well, then strain into 4 coupes. Top up with a splash of well-chilled ginger beer, then finish with the fennel fronds and flowers.

For a longer drink, pour into lowball glasses filled with ice and top with a larger serving of ginger beer.

Margarita Picante

Makes 2

4 fine slices of red chilli
   (with or without seeds
   depending on how hot you
   like it)
1 tsp coriander seeds
ice
90 g (3¼ oz/6 tbsps) tequila
60 g (2¼ oz/4 tbsps) lime
   juice
30 g (1 oz/2 tbsps) agave
   syrup
coriander (cilantro) leaves,
   to garnish *(optional)*

SUBS
agave – honey
red chilli – any fresh chilli
   you enjoy

Strong and spicy for those evenings when only tequila will do.

In a pestle and mortar, bash 2 slices of the chilli together with the coriander seeds until roughly broken down (it does not need to be fine). Add to a shaker with some ice and the other ingredients. Shake well for 1 minute.

Strain into 2 small glasses or tumblers filled with ice (a giant single ice cube is great here). Garnish with the last of the chilli slices (or a whole chilli, if you're feeling brave) and a coriander leaf.

Rhubarb Shrub

Makes 1–1.5 L (4–6 cups)

500 g (1 lb 2 oz) rhubarb

500 g (1 lb 2 oz/2 generous
    cups) caster (superfine)
    sugar

150 g (5 oz/scant ⅔ cup)
    water

small piece of fresh ginger

250 g (9 oz/1 cup) white
    wine vinegar

TO SERVE

ice

sparkling water

SUBS

rhubarb – gooseberries;
    brambles; peaches;
    apples; plums

caster sugar – light brown
    sugar will give an almost
    caramel-like flavour

ginger – herbs such as mint,
    thyme or basil will work too

This is a slightly adapted shrub recipe, as it is cooked and contains less vinegar than normal. Most shrubs involve macerating the fruit with sugar overnight, then adding an equal part of vinegar. To my taste, this is a little too strong, so here I have included less for a more versatile flavour. I prefer cooking the fruit for this, as it helps bring out the ginger flavour too. You can swap the rhubarb out for gooseberries, brambles and peaches if you want to make shrubs when rhubarb is out of season. This is also great when added to a gin and tonic.

Roughly chop the rhubarb and place in a large saucepan with the sugar and water. Slice the ginger into thick pieces and add to the pan. Cook over a medium heat until the rhubarb has cooked down and softened. Remove from the heat and stir in the vinegar. Allow to infuse for 30 minutes.

Strain through a jelly bag or muslin-lined colander. Store in a sterilised bottle in the refrigerator for up to 1 month.

To serve, pour 50 g (2 oz/3 tbsps) shrub over ice, then top up with sparkling water.

Gooseberry *and* Tonic

Makes 2

FOR THE SYRUP

100 g (3½ oz) gooseberries

100 g (3½ oz/scant ½ cup)
water

100 g (3½ oz/scant ½ cup)
caster (superfine) sugar

TO SERVE

60 g (2¼ oz/¼ cup) gin
(optional)

60 g (2¼ oz/¼ cup)
gooseberry syrup (see
above)

1½ tbsps lime juice

12 mint leaves

ice

tonic water, to top up

SUBS

gooseberries – red
gooseberries; brambles;
blackcurrants

lime – lemon juice

mint – sorrel or basil

tonic – soda water

I love this as both a boozy and non-boozy cocktail. The gin can easily be omitted from the recipe, and you will still end up with a sophisticated and refreshing drink for a summer's afternoon.

Bring all of the ingredients for the syrup to the boil in a small saucepan. Stir to make sure everything is dissolved and the gooseberries are just beginning to soften. Set aside to infuse for 30 minutes. Strain the syrup and store in a glass jar or bottle in the refrigerator for up to 2 weeks.

If you are making the cocktails on the same day, reserve 2 tsps of the strained gooseberries. Alternatively, any excess gooseberries can be used in a compote, served with some granola and yoghurt, or spooned on top of a cake or pavlova.

In a jar, muddle together the gin, if using, syrup and lime juice and 6 mint leaves with some ice. Divide the reserved gooseberries from making the syrup between 2 highball glasses, then fill with ice. Add 3 mint leaves to each glass. Strain the syrup mix between the glasses, then top up with tonic and serve.

MID-WEEK MENUS

TO EAT

Courgette and Lemon Pasta
with Almonds, pg. 25

Pesto
(Toast 20 g/¾ oz flaked/slivered almonds
and 20 g/¾ oz sunflower seeds in a pan
until golden. Blitz in a food processor
with 1 garlic clove, 40 g/1½ oz grated
pecorino, 120 g/4 oz/½ cup good olive
oil, 80 g/3 oz basil, parsley and fennel
fronds, and some salt and pepper. Keep
in the refrigerator for up to 1 week.)

Focaccia

TO DRINK

Vermouth and Tonic
(Fill a lowball glass with lots of ice, then
pour over 2 tbsps of vermouth, top up
with 5 tbsps of tonic, then finish with
3 nocellara olives and a wee splash of
brine. If you are not drinking booze, this
works very well with a non-alcoholic
spirit, such as Pentire or Seedlip.)

TO EAT

Turmeric and Tahini Dressing with
Potatoes, pg. 144

Avocado Dressing with Baby Gem
Lettuce, pg. 145

Spiced Almonds, pg. 94

TO DRINK

Apple Spritz
(Place some ice in a small wine glass
or coupe, then pour over 3 tbsps of apple
juice. Add a slice of fresh ginger and
muddle together. Top up with 100 g/
3½ oz/scant ½ cup of a plain or ginger
kombucha. Finish with a slice of apple.)

TO EAT

Butterbeans, Artichoke and Steak,
pg. 58

Quick Chocolate Mousse
pg. 167

TO DRINK

Vodka Fizz, pg. 78

TO EAT

Halloumi, Melon and Tomato Salad
with Chilli, pg. 28

Meringues with Apricots and Saffron
(Allow for 1 small meringue per person.
Slice 2 apricots per person in half and
remove the stone. Heat 100 g/3½ oz/
scant ½ cup caster/superfine sugar with
5 tbsps of water and a few strands of
saffron. Bring to the boil, then add the
apricots. Cook for a few minutes until
you have a syrup-like consistency. Break
the meringues into rough chunks and
arrange on the plate. Add a spoonful of
good full-fat yoghurt, then spoon over the
apricots and saffron syrup. Garnish with
some chopped toasted skin-on almonds.)

TO DRINK

Margarita Picante, pg. 83

or

Cucumber Agua Fresca
(Blitz together 100 g/3½ oz peeled
cucumber with 200 g/7 oz/scant 1 cup
water, juice of ½ lime, 1 tsp agave syrup
– or to taste – and a few mint leaves.
Once smooth, pour over ice and serve.)

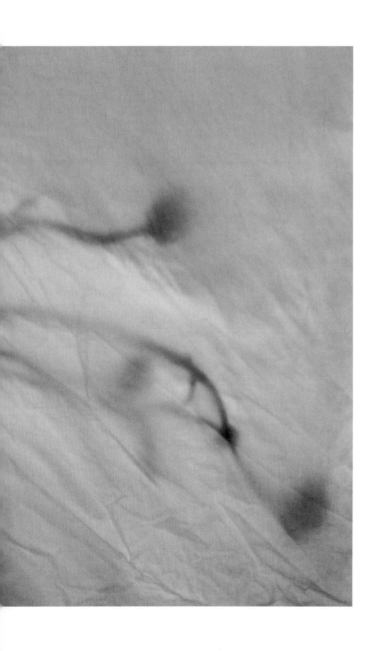

GOOD THINGS TO DRINK (AND EAT!)

Grapes, Fennel *and* Burrata

*Serves 4 as a drinks
   accompaniment*

1 large fennel bulb (about
   250 g/9 oz), fronds
   reserved
250 g (9 oz) mixed grapes
2 tsps cider vinegar
½ tsp fennel seeds
a glug of olive oil
150 g (5 oz) burrata
extra virgin olive oil,
   for drizzling
30 g (1 oz) toasted flaked
   (slivered) almonds
salt and freshly ground
   black pepper
toasted sourdough or
   crackers, to serve

SUBS
burrata – labneh
fennel fronds – dill
almonds – toasted
   sunflower seeds; toasted
   hazelnuts

I suppose this is the lighter version of a cheese board.
Although not traditionally served pre-dinner, it does
make for an excellent dish to share with a bottle of
something delicious.

Preheat the oven to 200°C fan (430°F/gas 8).

Chop the fennel into 1 cm (½ in) strips lengthways and
arrange on a roasting dish (pan) with the grapes (stalks
attached), vinegar, fennel seeds, a good glug of oil and some
salt and pepper. Mix together, ensuring everything is well
coated. Roast for 20 minutes, or until the fennel is softened
and everything is golden and sticky. Set aside to cool.

To serve, spoon the roasted fennel and grapes onto a large
plate alongside the burrata.

Drizzle with extra virgin olive oil, season with more salt
and pepper, and garnish with the fennel fronds and some
toasted flaked almonds. Serve with some toasted sourdough
or crackers.

Fried Olives

*Serves 4 as a drinks
accompaniment*

50 g (2 oz) anchovy fillets
3 tbsps olive oil (I use the
    oil from the anchovy tin
    alongside olive oil here)
35 g (1¼ oz) grated
    Parmesan
1 garlic clove
1 tbsp lemon juice
¼ tsp freshly ground black
    pepper
5 g (¼ oz) chervil
about 300 g (10½ oz)
    (drained weight) medium
    pitted green olives
    (referred to as Queen
    olives)
50 g (2 oz/scant ½ cup)
    plain (all-purpose) flour
2–3 eggs
150 g (5 oz/2½ cups) panko
    breadcrumbs
salt and freshly ground
    black pepper
sunflower or vegetable oil,
    for deep-frying

SUBS
Parmesan – Grana Padano
chervil – parsley
panko – stale sourdough,
    blitzed until fine

Deep fried olives are frequently served in New York cocktail bars, and despite craving a visit to a New York cocktail bar, I've never made it to one. I made these one evening and we ate a mammoth amount of them washed down by numerous Old Fashioneds (recipe on page 128).

In a food processor, blitz the anchovies, oil, Parmesan, garlic, lemon juice, pepper and chervil to a smooth paste. Transfer to a piping bag fitted with a small round nozzle.

Drain the olives and shake off any excess liquid. Pipe the filling into the centre of the olives, filling them until just below the top (overfilling will make them harder to fry). Set aside.

Place the flour in a shallow bowl and season well, stirring to combine. Crack the eggs into a second shallow bowl and whisk lightly. Place the panko breadcrumbs into a third bowl. One by one, coat the stuffed olives in flour, dusting off the excess, then coat them in the egg before rolling in the breadcrumbs. Set aside in a tray until all of the olives are coated. This is quite a fiddly process, but I promise it is worth it!

Half-fill a large saucepan with oil and heat it to 180°C/356°F. Once at temperature, fry the olives in batches for 2–3 minutes or until golden brown. Remove with a slotted spoon to drain on kitchen paper.

Serve warm and when still crisp!

Spiced Almonds

Makes 500 g (1 lb 2 oz)

1 tbsp black peppercorns
2 tsps cumin seeds
½ tsp habañero chilli flakes
   (or ancho if you prefer a
   slightly milder heat)
½ tsp ground turmeric
1 tsp ground coriander
2 tsps Maldon sea salt
1 tbsp caster (superfine)
   sugar
1 tsp nigella seeds
1 egg white
500 g (1 lb 2 oz) whole skin-
   on almonds
extra virgin olive oil, for
   drizzling

SUBS
nigella seeds – black
   sesame seeds
sugar – honey
egg white – olive oil (this
   will make the recipe
   vegan-friendly)

These have been on my Christmas bake list for years and are often wrapped up in little cellophane bags tied with velvet ribbon as gifts. I recently decided that they were so tasty and easy to make that it was a shame to keep them solely for festivities. Make a large batch of these and store in an airtight container for spontaneous drinks and snacking.

Preheat the oven to 190°C fan (410°F/gas 7).

In a pestle and mortar or a food processor, bash/blitz the peppercorns until coarse. Add the cumin, chilli, turmeric, coriander, salt, sugar and nigella seeds and blitz again until you have a rough powder. Mix the spice powder with the egg white and the almonds until they're all evenly coated.

Tip onto a baking tray (pan) and roast in the oven for 5 minutes. Remove from the oven, shake and mix to make sure everything is evenly coated, then roast for another 5 minutes.

Repeat this once or twice more, or until the almonds are golden and fragrant and the mixture is well distributed – be careful not to burn the nuts.

Once cooked, drizzle with a little extra virgin olive oil while still hot and toss together.

Set aside to cool before storing in an airtight container. The nuts will keep like this for up to 3 weeks.

Crackers

Makes 16–20 large crackers, for breaking into smaller shards

150 g (5 oz/1¼ cups) plain (all-purpose) flour, plus extra for dusting

100 g (3½ oz/¾ cup) white spelt flour

100 g (3½ oz/scant ½ cup) water

40 g (1½ oz/scant 3 tbsps) olive oil, plus extra for brushing

1 tsp honey

½ tsp Maldon sea salt, plus extra to garnish

½ tsp freshly ground black pepper

1 tbsp white sesame seeds

1 tbsp black sesame seeds

1 tbsp poppy seeds

Salty and seedy, these make a great addition to a cheese board or when served with some pâté or dips before a meal. You could even serve them for both and bookend your meal with crackers!

Place all the ingredients in a bowl and mix together with your hands. If the dough is very dry, add another small splash of water, but don't overdo it as you want to dough to be quite firm. Once the dough forms, cover the bowl and place in the refrigerator for 2 hours.

Preheat the oven to 190°C fan (410°F/gas 7).

Divide the dough into quarters, then quarters or fifths again. On a lightly floured work surface, roll a piece out as thinly as you can. Cover with a clean dish towel and set aside before repeating the same thing with another 3–4 balls. Return to the first cracker and roll out again – it should stretch further now it has relaxed a little. Once about 1 mm thick (or as thin as possible without breaking), place on a baking tray (pan) lined with baking paper. Brush each cracker with some olive oil, then sprinkle with sea salt flakes.

Bake for 5–10 minutes, or until golden brown and cooked through. After 5 minutes, I check them regularly, so they don't burn.

Repeat the process with the rest of the dough. Once cooled, break up the crackers into shards and store them in an airtight container for up to 1 month.

Spinach *and* Artichoke Dip

*Serves 4–6 as a drinks
    accompaniment*

250 g (9 oz) fresh spinach
    (this will cook down to
    about 100 g/3½ oz)
2 medium banana shallots,
    finely sliced
3–4 garlic cloves, crushed
a drizzle of olive oil
25 g (¾ oz) flat-leaf parsley,
    finely chopped, plus extra
    to garnish
1 tsp Maldon sea salt
freshly ground black pepper
½–1 tsp Aleppo pepper
    (optional)
150 g (5 oz) artichokes in oil
    (drained weight)
250 g (9 oz) cream cheese
50 g (2 oz/3 tbsps) double
    (heavy) cream
extra virgin olive oil, for
    drizzling

SUBS

spinach – I don't recommend
    subbing the whole amount
    of spinach, but if you are
    short on weight you can
    top up with rocket
    (arugula), more parsley,
    chervil or sorrel
Aleppo pepper – ¼ tsp chilli
    (hot pepper) flakes mixed
    with ¼ tsp smoked paprika
double cream – cream
    cheese; full-fat yoghurt

This dip is the result of many attempts to try and recreate the version on offer at The Pulitzer Bar in Amsterdam. We visited one January and inhaled this dip with toasted flatbreads. It was served warm and was truly one of the best drink accompaniments I have ever had.

Begin by frying the spinach in a large dry frying pan (skillet) over a medium heat until the spinach wilts down. Drain the leaves over a colander and allow to cool for 10 minutes.

Once cool enough to handle, squeeze the spinach to get rid of any excess moisture. Place the spinach in a food processor and set aside.

In the same pan, gently fry the banana shallots and garlic in a little olive oil. Cook until softened but try not to colour the onions.

Add to the food processor alongside the spinach and blitz for a minute or so until smooth. Add the parsley, salt, a little black pepper, and the Aleppo pepper (if using). Blitz again until combined. Add the artichokes and blitz again until smooth, making sure you scrape down the sides of the processor with a spatula. The mix should no longer be too warm but if it is still hot, set aside for 15 minutes to allow to cool down. If it is too hot the mix will split and become runny. Once cooled, add the cream cheese and double cream and blitz to a fairly smooth paste.

When ready to serve, spoon onto a platter and serve with a generous drizzle of extra virgin olive oil, some chopped parsley and a generous amount of black pepper. Enjoy with crackers, flatbreads or toast. It will keep in the refrigerator for up to 2 days.

GOOD THINGS TO DRINK (AND EAT!)

Romesco

Serves 4-6

35 g (1¼ oz) sourdough
20 g (¾ oz/2 generous
    tbsps) hazelnuts
20 g (¾ oz) whole almonds
100 g (3½ oz) roasted red
    peppers, from a jar
1 garlic clove
1 tsp smoked paprika
1 tbsp sherry vinegar
about 100 g (3½ oz/scant
    ½ cup) olive oil
salt and freshly ground
    black pepper

SUBS

jarred peppers – you can
    char the same weight of
    fresh peppers over a
    flame until blackened,
    cover and allow to sit for
    10 minutes, then peel off
    the blackened skin (it's
    okay to leave a little on)
    and remove the seeds
almonds – more hazelnuts;
    walnuts; macadamias
sherry – red or white wine
    vinegar

I make romesco quite regularly and the best one I have ever tried was from Noble Rot in London. They topped it with a whole burrata and some charred spring onions (scallions). It was heaven and I would encourage you to do the same.

Preheat the oven to 190°C fan (410°F/gas 7).

Tear the bread into rough chunks and arrange over a baking tray (pan). Add the nuts and roast for 5–7 minutes or until the nuts are golden and fragrant, and the bread has crisped up.

Place in a food processor and blitz on a high speed until coarsely chopped. Add the peppers, garlic, paprika and vinegar, and blitz again until well combined. With the motor still running, pour in the oil in a steady stream. You may need to stop and scrape down the side occasionally. If the mix is too dry, add a little more oil. Season to taste.

Store in the refrigerator for up to 1 week.

Buttered Leek Croquettes

Makes 30–35 croquettes

400 g (14 oz) leeks, finely
   chopped
a drizzle of olive oil
125 g (4 oz) butter
75 g (2½ oz/½ cup)
   wholemeal flour, plus
   extra for dusting
400 g (14 oz/generous 1½
   cups) milk
25 g (¾ oz) Parmesan, finely
   grated
100 g (3½ oz) crème fraîche
¼ tsp finely grated nutmeg
75 g (2½ oz) Cheddar,
   grated
2 tsps poppy seeds
2 eggs
300 g (10½ oz/5 cups)
   panko breadcrumbs
salt and freshly ground
   black pepper
sunflower oil, for deep-
   frying

SUBS

wholemeal flour – spelt flour;
   plain (all-purpose) flour
crème fraîche – cream
Cheddar – Gruyère would be
   a nice alternative
panko – stale bread, blitzed

This makes a lot of croquettes but somehow whenever I make them it's simply never enough. I tend to make the filling the night before for these, and then shape and coat in the morning, before frying to order. Frying can take a bit of time, so do make sure to plan your main dish around this – they are worth the effort!

Fry the leeks in 50 g (2 oz) of the butter in a large saucepan over a medium heat. You want to soften them rather than colour them. Season with salt and pepper.

In a separate saucepan, heat the remaining butter and flour together, cook for a few minutes, then add the milk, bit by bit, whisking in between to make a thick béchamel sauce. Whisk in the Parmesan, crème fraîche, nutmeg and Cheddar until smooth and glossy. Remove from the heat and season to taste. Stir in the poppy seeds and the softened leeks and pour into a shallow dish. Cover and cool for 1 hour, then place in the refrigerator to chill down completely (ideally 1–2 hours or overnight).

When ready to fry, lay out 3 shallow bowls: one filled with some flour, seasoned well; one with the eggs, whisked together; and one with the panko breadcrumbs. Roll the chilled mixture into small bite-size balls, then dust in a little flour. Shake off any excess, then roll in the egg mixture, and lastly coat in the breadcrumbs. Place on a plate and repeat until the leek mixture is used up. Pop in the refrigerator to firm up a little if you find the croquettes are getting soft. They can also be frozen at this stage for frying at a later date.

Half-fill a large saucepan with oil and heat it to 170°C/338°F. Once at temperature, carefully fry the croquettes in batches,

making sure not to overcrowd the pan. Fry for a few minutes before turning to get an even colour all over. Remove from the pan with a slotted spoon once golden brown (roughly 3–4 minutes but maybe more if you have made larger croquettes). Drain on some kitchen paper.

Eat as soon as possible. These are great served with a little sea salt, grated Parmesan and a sprinkling of paprika.

CHAPTER FOUR

Candlelight

Spiced Lamb *with* Hummus

*Feeds 2 as a main or 4 as a
side/starter*

FOR THE MARINATED LAMB

1 tsp dried mint

1 tsp dried oregano

1 tsp ground cinnamon

1 tsp salt

1 tsp sumac

1 tsp mixed spice

2 tbsps olive oil

zest of ½ lemon

500 g (1 lb 2 oz) good-quality
    lamb neck, ideally in 2 or
    3 fillets, sinew removed

FOR THE HUMMUS

1 × 400 g (14 oz) tin
chickpeas (garbanzo
beans), drained (see note on
    page 107)

50 g (2 oz/3 tbsps) tahini

25 g (¾ oz/1¾ tbsps) lemon
    juice

1 garlic clove

25 g (¾ oz/1¾ tbsps) extra
    virgin olive oil

25 g (¾ oz) ice

¾ tsp salt

¾ tsp black pepper

FOR THE HERB OIL

10 g (½ oz) flat-leaf parsley,
    chopped

10 g (½ oz) dill, chopped

10 g (½ oz) mint, chopped

zest of ½ lemon

25 g (¾ oz/1¾ tbsps) lemon
    juice

As a long-term hummus decorator, I love to add extra bits of spice, crunch and flavour to my chickpeas. This is perhaps taking it a bit too far, but the result is a wonderfully versatile dinner dish.

Begin by marinating the lamb. Place all the ingredients in a bowl and massage into the lamb. Cover with clingfilm (plastic wrap) and marinate for 30 minutes–1 hour in the refrigerator. Remove 10–20 minutes before cooking to come up to room temperature.

For the hummus, place the chickpeas, tahini, lemon juice and garlic in a food processor and blitz on a high speed until smooth and well combined. Mix the oil and ice together and gently pour into the hummus with the motor still running. Add the seasoning, blitz and taste, adjusting if necessary. Continue to blitz for another 2 minutes until smooth.

To prepare the herb oil, mix together the parsley, dill, mint and lemon zest. I like to rub the zest in with the herbs to release the oils. Add the lemon juice and the oil and mix together, seasoning a little. In a dry frying pan (skillet), toast the sesame seeds until fragrant and just beginning to colour. Add to the oil and set aside.

When ready to cook the lamb, preheat an ovenproof frying pan over a medium-high heat. Preheat your oven to 180°C fan (400°F/gas 6). Place the lamb neck into the hot pan and sear on all sides until golden brown, 3–4 minutes. Reduce the heat and continue to cook the lamb, turning it regularly until the central temperature is 65–70°C/149–158°F for medium-rare, or to your taste. Once the lamb is seared, you can place it in the oven for another 5–10 minutes, but I prefer the char you get from pan-frying. When cooked to your liking, remove

25 g (¾ oz/1¾ tbsps) extra
virgin olive oil
10 g (½ oz/1 tbsp) sesame
seeds
salt and freshly ground
black pepper

SUBS
chickpeas – butter (lima)
beans
dried oregano – dried thyme;
dried marjoram
parsley – chervil
dill – fennel fronds
sesame – flaked (slivered)
almonds; poppy seeds

from the pan and place on a plate. Cover with foil or another plate, then place a dish towel on top. Rest for 5–10 minutes – the longer the better.

When ready to serve, spoon the hummus onto your serving platter. I like to use the back of the spoon to create lots of swirls. Slice your lamb into rounds and arrange over the top of the hummus. Spoon over any resting juices. Finish with the herb oil and any extra herb leaves you fancy.

Eat immediately with some flatbreads, the Spiced Almonds on page 94, and the Pickled Radish, Fennel and Chicory Salad on page 161. This also makes a nice additional dish to accompany the Lamb with Aubergine on page 114 if you want to create an epic lamb feast.

NOTE
If you are looking for a silky and velvety-textured hummus, you can go one step further and remove the skins from the chickpeas. The best way to do this is to drain the chickpeas, wash them in warm water and rub them together between your hands. Continue to do this until the papery skins come loose. They should float to the top of the water, so you can scoop them out. Drain and repeat until all the skins have been removed. This isn't essential and really does take a fair amount of patience and time, but it does result in an amazing hummus if you can be bothered!

Tortellini *in* Brodo

*Makes 30–36 tortellini
(serves 4)*

FOR THE PASTA

200 g (7 oz/generous 1½
cups) '00' flour

2 eggs

2 tsps water, if needed (or
white wine as a lovely
nonna Regina once
taught me)

FOR THE FILLING

175 g (6 oz) ricotta

1 egg yolk

20 g (¾ oz) herbs (any mix
of parsley, basil, chives,
marjoram and oregano
will work well)

nutmeg, for grating

50 g (2 oz) Parmesan, finely
grated, plus extra to serve

salt and freshly ground
black pepper

TO FINISH

1 egg, beaten

flour or semolina, for dusting

1 kg (2 lb 4 oz/4 cups)
good-quality chicken
stock (the Pipers Farm
one is my favourite or use
recipe on page 208 – also
see note opposite)

10–15 g (½ oz) flat-leaf
parsley and marjoram
leaves

Parmesan, for grating

Handmade pasta is one of those things that always sounds like a good idea, but the reality of rolling and shaping enough tortellini for any number above 4 is very time-consuming. The perfect number of people to cater for is 2–4, as just about the time you lose interest in shaping you are finished!

In a food processor, blitz together the flour and eggs until a dough forms. If the mixture remains quite sandy, add some water. Remove from the processor and knead together, then cover with clingfilm (plastic wrap) or place in an airtight container. Leave to rest for at least 30 minutes at room temperature, or ideally 2 hours or overnight in the refrigerator. If you have rested the dough in the refrigerator, allow it to come to room temperature for 15 minutes before working.

To make the filling, place the ricotta, egg yolk and herbs in a food processor and blitz to a smooth, pale green mixture. Transfer to a bowl, grate over a little nutmeg and add the Parmesan. Season with salt and pepper and stir well. This can be stored in the refrigerator for up to 2 days.

Once your pasta dough has been rested, divide into quarters. Cover 3 pieces and begin to roll out the first one. Everyone's pasta machine is different, so please bear this in mind when working with your dough. My machine's widest setting is '0', so I take my dough to setting 8 for tortellini as this is a little thinner than I use for tagliatelle (setting 7) and allows for the dough to be folded over on itself. You may want to double the dough over itself and roll through each setting again, however I find the dough is just as good if it isn't folded over itself and rolled through each thickness twice before being reduced again.

extra virgin olive oil, for
   drizzling

SUBS

ricotta – mascarpone

Parmesan – Grana Padano;
   pecorino

chicken stock – veggie
   stock

NOTE

If you want a crystal-clear
stock, you can clarify it
by whisking an egg white
into the hot stock. Bring to
the boil and cook for a few
minutes, then strain through
a muslin-lined sieve.

When your dough is thin enough, cut out 9 cm (3½ in) circles with a round plain cutter. Spoon small amounts (about a teaspoonful) of the filling into the middle of each disc. Brush the bottom half of the dough with a little beaten egg (too much will make the shaping harder, so use sparingly). Fold over the top half, being careful not to squeeze out any filling. Use the side of your little finger to press the dough down in a semi-circle shape. Lift up the corners of the semi-circle and wrap them around to meet each other. Use your thumb and forefinger to join them together, pressing firmly to seal. Place your tortellini on a tray dusted with a little flour or semolina.

Repeat the process with the rest of the dough. Any scraps of dough can be scrunched together, covered in clingfilm, and rested for another 20–30 minutes. I re-roll these to create more tortellini. Purists would say this is criminal but I have never been able to tell the difference between those re-rolled and those on the first roll. Resting the dough in between is crucial though. Compost any scraps.

Allow your pasta shapes to dry a little at room temperature for 1 hour, or in an airtight container in the refrigerator overnight (line the container with more flour and make sure your tortellini are not touching each other in case they stick). If you are making these ahead of time, simply freeze them in the same way as you would store in the refrigerator. Once frozen, you can condense them to a smaller airtight tub as they will not stick together when solid. Cook from frozen as usual, but allow an additional 2 minutes' cooking time.

To cook, bring your stock to the boil in a large pan (see note). Season a little, then add your tortellini. Cook for 5–6 minutes, or until the pasta is just cooked. Remove from the heat and stir in your picked herb leaves.

Serve in a shallow bowl, with a grating of Parmesan, black pepper and a drizzle of extra virgin olive oil.

Pork Shoulder
with Rhubarb Ketchup

Serves 4

1 kg (2 lb 4 oz) high-welfare
   pork shoulder, skin-on,
   deboned
150 g (5 oz/scant ⅔ cup)
   white wine
300 g (10½ oz/1¼ cups)
   vegetable or pork stock,
   or as needed
4 banana shallots
4 celery stalks
4 rosemary sprigs
4 bay leaves
4 fresh thyme sprigs
salt and freshly ground
   black pepper

FOR THE RHUBARB
   KETCHUP
2 banana shallots, finely
   chopped
a drizzle of olive oil
2 garlic cloves, finely sliced
400 g (14 oz) fresh rhubarb,
   chopped into roughly 2cm
   (3¼ in) pieces
100 g (3½ oz/scant ½ cup)
   caster (superfine) sugar
50 g (2 oz/scant ⅓ cup) light
   brown sugar
150 g (5 oz/scant ⅔ cup)
   white wine vinegar or
   cider vinegar
½ tsp ground ground ginger
½ tsp ground coriander
½ tsp salt

Most people would start with the meat when recipe writing, but if I am being honest this dish came about because I wanted to serve this ketchup with something other than a bacon sandwich (even though it makes an excellent bacon sandwich). Pork belly is just as good.

Preheat the oven to 140°C fan (275°F/gas 1).

Season the pork shoulder generously with salt and pepper and place into a snug but deep roasting tin (pan). I like to roll the shoulder out flat, but skin-side up, for this. Pour the white wine and stock around the meat (don't use it all if it will fully submerge the meat – you want the liquid to be about halfway up the side of the meat when it is laid out flat). Cover the tin securely with foil and roast in the oven for 3 hours, checking every 30 minutes or so and basting with the juices.

Quarter the shallots and cut the celery into 5–7 cm (2–3 in) pieces. Remove the foil from the pork, add the vegetables along with the herbs, and cook for a further 1 hour, being careful not to dry out the meat (top up with more stock if the tin is dry).

Meanwhile, move onto the rhubarb ketchup. In a medium saucepan with a lid, sweat down the shallots in a little olive oil for 5–10 minutes over a medium heat. Add the garlic and cook for another few minutes. Add the rhubarb and reduce the heat to low, cover and allow the rhubarb to cook down and lose its shape entirely, making sure you stir regularly to stop it sticking. When softened, add the sugars, vinegar, spices and salt, and stir to combine. Bring to the boil over a medium heat with the lid off for 5–10 minutes.

SUBS

rhubarb – plums; cooked
   beetroot (beets)
white wine – more stock
celery – 150 g (5 oz) leeks or
   fennel

You should notice the mixture thickens up quite a bit. Place the rhubarb ketchup in a food processor and blitz until smooth. At this point, you can either serve as is or you can return it to the pan and boil a little to further reduce it down and get more of a jammy consistency. Set aside to cool, then store in the refrigerator until ready to serve.

When ready to serve, place the roasted pork shoulder on a deep platter and spoon over the juices and vegetables. Serve with a bowl of the ketchup, some nice new potatoes and a plate of the mustardy French bean recipe on page 153.

Any excess ketchup will keep in an airtight container in the refrigerator for 1–2 weeks and is very delicious on bacon sandwiches!

Lamb *with* Aubergine

Serves 4

1–1.5 kg (2 lb 4 oz–3 lb 5 oz)
  high-welfare lamb
  shoulder, bone in
1 large garlic bulb
2 aubergines (eggplant)
zest and juice of ½ lemon
25 g (¾ oz) flat-leaf parsley,
  finely chopped, plus extra
  to garnish
extra virgin olive oil, for
  drizzling
15 g (½ oz) toasted pumpkin
  seeds, finely chopped
vegetable stock *(optional)*

FOR THE LAMB MARINADE
15 g (½ oz) coriander
  (cilantro) stalks and all
15 g (½ oz) flat-leaf parsley
  stalks and all
1 tsp paprika
75 g (2½ oz/5 tbsps) olive oil
1 tsp sumac
1 tsp cumin seeds
1 tsp sea salt
zest and juice of 1 lemon
salt and freshly ground
  black pepper

SUBS
coriander – chervil; dill
sumac – zest of ½ lemon
cumin seeds – ½ tsp ground
  cumin
pumpkin seeds – sunflower
  seeds

This is a fairly long-winded way of making a great baba ganoush, but I promise it's worth it. Effort-wise the dish has a fairly hands-off approach, which I love for a feast menu as I can turn to sides and puds (my favourites).

First, prepare the marinade. Place all the ingredients in a food processor and blitz to a paste. Massage the paste over the lamb shoulder and place in a deep but snug-fitting roasting tin (pan). Cover and refrigerate overnight.

The next day, preheat the oven to 150°C fan (340°F/gas 3). If you have the time, allow the marinated lamb to come to room temperature for 30 mintues. Cover the marinated lamb with foil and roast in the oven for 1.5 hours. Remove from the oven and add the garlic bulb, skin and all, then return to the oven for a further 1.5 hours, still covered.

Meanwhile, char the aubergines over a gas flame so that they get nicely blackened and blistered. You can also do this over a barbecue or under a hot grill (broiler).

Remove the lamb from the oven, discard the foil and add the aubergines to the tin. Reduce the oven to 140°C fan (320°F/gas 2). Roast for a final 1.5 hours. Make sure you check the dish regularly and baste with any juices to stop it from drying out. If the tin does dry out, you can add a little bit of vegetable stock and continue to cook and baste with that.Once cooked, the meat should be soft, succulent and falling away from the bone. Cover and allow to rest for 10 minutes.

Scoop the flesh from the aubergines and place in a bowl, then squeeze the soft garlic cloves out of their skins into the bowl. Discard the skins. Mix together with a fork to break

everything up. Add the lemon zest and juice, and parsley, and season to taste. Add a spoonful of any cooking juices.

Tip the aubergine dip onto a serving plate and spoon out in a nice swirl. Drizzle generously with extra virgin olive oil and top with some chopped parsley and chopped pumpkin seeds. Serve alongside the lamb. This dish also goes very well with the Green Bulgur Wheat on page 156.

Roasted Spatchcock Chicken
with Herb Mayo

Serves 4

1 medium free-range
   chicken (ideally 1.5–1.75 kg/
   3 lb 5 oz–3 lb 14 oz)
1 lemon, quartered
1 whole garlic bulb, halved
   widthways
1 large onion or 2 banana
   shallots, quartered
100 g (3½ oz/scant ½ cup)
   white wine
50 g (2 oz) unsalted butter,
   softened
3 tbsps olive oil
25 g (¾ oz) flat-leaf parsley
1 tsp salt
1 tsp cracked black pepper

FOR THE HERB MAYO
1 egg
½ tsp grainy mustard
½ tsp caster (superfine)
   sugar
1 tsp salt
½ tsp freshly ground black
   pepper
1 garlic clove, crushed,
   or 4 roasted garlic cloves
   from the chicken
200 g (7 oz/scant 1 cup)
   sunflower oil
2 tsps lemon juice
10 g (½ oz) flat-leaf parsley

SUBS
grainy mustard – Dijon
   mustard

A lot of butter and booze will always make for a good chicken recipe. It could maybe even be said that there is not quite enough in this recipe …!

Preheat the oven to 180°C fan (400°F/gas 6).

To spatchcock the chicken, place it on your chopping board, breast-side down. Use your fingers to identify the spine. Place the tip of a large sharp knife to one side of the spine and cut down through the ribs, being careful not to damage the breasts below. Repeat on the other side, then give the bird a half turn and repeat on both sides again. (If you have a good pair of butcher's scissors, you can simply snip the spine out on both sides.) Flip the chicken over and press down in the middle of the breasts to flatten. Place in a deep roasting dish or tin (pan), ideally one suitable for serving in. Arrange the lemon, garlic and onion around the chicken.

In a food processor, combine the wine, butter, oil, parsley and seasoning, and blitz for 3 minutes, or until smooth. Don't worry if the mixture looks like it's curdled, continue to blitz and a paste will eventually form.

Massage the paste evenly over the top of the chicken skin. Roast for about 1.5 hours, or until cooked through. You want to baste every 30 minutes or so to prevent the chicken and garlic cloves from drying out. When cooked, remove from the oven and let rest for 10 minutes.

Meanwhile, begin making the mayonnaise. Place the egg, mustard, sugar, salt and pepper in a food processor and blitz to a paste. If you are using the punchier raw garlic (rather than the roasted cloves), add it now and ensure it gets well distributed. With the motor still running, trickle in the

caster sugar – honey

sunflower oil – vegetable oil

parsley – chervil; coriander
 (cilantro)

sunflower oil, a little at a time. You can do this by hand with a whisk and bowl, but it will take longer! If you're using the roasted garlic, simply squeeze it out of the cloves and mash it up a little with a fork, then whisk it into the mayonnaise. Finally, whisk in the lemon juice and finely chopped parsley.

Serve the chicken dish and the herb mayo with some new potatoes. This is also a good match for the Buttered Leek Croquettes on page 100.

Lemon Sole *with* Samphire, Hazelnuts *and* Capers

Serves 2

3 tbsps plain (all-purpose) flour

1 tsp salt

about ½ tsp freshly ground black pepper

1 whole lemon sole, skinned and gutted or 2 fillets

35 g (1¼ oz/¼ cup) hazelnuts

75 g (2½ oz) butter, cubed

zest of ¼ lemon plus juice of whole lemon

1–2 tbsps capers

25 g (¾ oz) samphire

10 g (½ oz) fennel fronds, finely chopped

10 g (½ oz) dill, finely chopped

sunflower oil, for cooking

SUBS

lemon sole – dover sole or another flat fish

hazelnuts – macadamia

fennel – chives

samphire – sea kale

A twist on the classic sole meunière, with the saltiness coming from both the samphire and the capers, I also love the texture provided by the hazelnuts.

Mix together the flour, salt and pepper on a plate large enough for the fish. Place the sole on top of the flour and coat both sides evenly, using your hands to cover any spots that are missed. This will help protect the fish when cooking and stop it from sticking to the pan. Dust off any excess.

Heat a large frying pan (skillet) over a medium-high heat. Add the hazelnuts to the pan and cook until fragrant and well toasted. Remove from the pan and chop roughly. Prepare all the other ingredients before cooking the fish, so everything is ready.

Add a little oil to the frying pan and return to a medium heat. You don't want the heat to be too fierce. When the oil is shimmering, add the fish. Cook on one side, shaking the pan occasionally to make sure it doesn't stick, until golden brown. Flip the fish carefully and cook on the other side for a few minutes. Timings will depend on size, so the best way to test if the fish is cooked is to insert a knife into the backbone to see if it will come away easily. Alternatively, probe the middle of the fish with a thermometer – you are looking for roughly 60°C (140°F) here. Remove from the pan to a warm serving plate.

Add the butter to the pan and allow to foam. Add the lemon zest, juice, capers and samphire mixing well. Cook for 30 seconds, then stir in the herbs, and chopped nuts and remove from the heat. Spoon over the fish and serve immediately.

SUPPER

Salt Beef *with* Shallots *and* Spiked Mayo

*Serves 4, with plenty of
extra beef for Reuben
sandwiches*

FOR THE BRINE

12 black peppercorns
1 tsp fennel seeds
1 tsp coriander seeds
1 tsp cumin seeds
2 kg (4 lb 8 oz/8 cups) water
250 g (9 oz/2 cups) fine salt
200 g (7 oz/generous 1 cup)
   dark muscovado sugar
2 thyme sprigs
2 rosemary sprigs
4 bay leaves
4 celery stalks

FOR THE SALT BEEF

2 kg (4 lb 8 oz) beef brisket,
   trimmed of excess fat
2 carrots, quartered
2 celery stalks, quartered
1 leek, quartered
1 garlic bulb, halved
   widthways

FOR THE MAYO

2 tbsps mayo
1 tbsp ketchup
1 tsp horseradish cream
a few dashes of
   Worcestershire sauce
¼ tsp paprika
salt and freshly ground
   black pepper

I started making salt beef after falling in love with the
Reuben sandwiches from Monty's Deli. Quickly we
decided we could not always wait for the beef to cool
down and slice (three days is already an investment) so
we enjoyed it one night served warm with some potatoes,
salad, and sauerkraut. It was delicious and thankfully
we still got to enjoy some Reuben sandwiches the
following day.

Place all of the brine ingredients, except the celery, into
a large saucepan and bring to the boil for 5 minutes. Cool
completely.

Place the celery in a food processor and blitz to a purée, then
stir it into the cold brine. This will help keep the meat pink.

In a large casserole dish or deep nonreactive roasting tray
(steel pan), place the brisket and cover with the brine. Make
sure it is fully submerged by weighing down with some plates,
if necessary. Cover and store in the refrigerator for 3 days
(or up to 5 days if required).

When ready to cook, preheat the oven to 170°C (340°F/gas 3).

Wash the brined meat thoroughly and discard the brine.
Clean the casserole dish or roasting tray and place the meat
back into it. Arrange the carrots, celery, leek and garlic
around it, then pour over enough water to cover. Tightly seal
or cover with foil and cook in the oven for about 4 hours,
or until the meat is tender and beginning to flake.

When the meat is nearly cooked, make the mayo. Mix together
the ingredients and season to taste.

FOR THE SHALLOTS

4 banana shallots,
    quartered
30 g (1 oz) butter
a drizzle of olive oil
2 thyme sprigs, leaves
    picked
5 g (¼ oz) flat-leaf parsley,
    finely chopped
salt and freshly ground
    black pepper

sauerkraut, to serve

Add the shallots to a saucepan over a medium heat. Allow to colour before adding the butter, a little oil and the picked thyme leaves. Cook slowly for 15 minutes until completely softened and beginning to colour. Season well and add the parsley just before serving.

To serve, remove the beef from the cooking liquid and slice a few generous pieces per person. Spoon the softened shallots onto plates and place the beef alongside it. Dollop on a little mayo per plate and serve with a small spoonful of sauerkraut for a sour kick.

This is also lovely with some simple boiled potatoes and a crunchy green salad.

Porchetta *with* Salsa Verde

Serves 4–6, with leftovers
for some extra tasty
sandwiches the next day

olive oil, for drizzling
2 kg (4 lb 8 oz) high-welfare
   pork loin with belly
   attached
200 g (7 oz) carrots, halved
   lengthways
200 g (7 oz) leeks, cut into
   5 cm (2 in) chunks
2 celery stalks, cut into 5 cm
   (2 in) chunks
100 g (3½ oz/scant ½ cup)
   white wine
salt and freshly ground
   black pepper

FOR THE STUFFING
olive oil, for cooking
2 large red onions, finely
   chopped
5 g (¼ oz) sage leaves, finely
   chopped
1 apple, grated
100 g (3½ oz) smoked
   streaky bacon, finely
   chopped
20 g (¾ oz) chives, finely
   chopped
4 garlic cloves, minced
100 g (3½ oz) sourdough
   bread
3 tbsps white wine
3 tbsps Vin Santo
1 tsp salt
½ tsp cracked black pepper

I once made a 12-kg (26 lb) version of this recipe and it was truly a mission! This is a more manageable quantity and is great to get in the oven on the morning of eating – your house will smell amazing for it. A great festive treat, it would make for a perfect and piggy Hogmanay supper.

Preheat the oven to 140°C fan (320°F/gas 2).

First, prepare the stuffing. Heat a little olive oil in a large frying pan (skillet) over a medium heat. Add the onions and sage leaves and cook until soft, then remove from the heat and place in a large bowl. Add the grated apple to the bowl.

Fry off the bacon in the same pan until cooked but not crispy. Add to the onion bowl and leave to cool down for 15 minutes.

Meanwhile, place the chives, garlic and bread in a food processor and blitz to fine breadcrumbs. Add these breadcrumbs to the now cool bacon and onion mixture, along with the white wine and Vin Santo. Add the salt and pepper, and ensure everything is evenly distributed and well combined.

Lay the pork out, skin-side up, on a large chopping board. Diagonally score the skin roughly halfway through the fat every few centimetres. Flip the pork over skin-side down and press flat. You may need to cut across the loin a little to flatten it fully. Scatter the stuffing mixture over the pork and use your hands to compact and spread it evenly across the surface of the meat. Roll up, loin side first, as tightly as you can and secure with butcher's string.

Place the roll in a deep roasting tray (pan), seam-side down. Drizzle the top with olive oil and season generously. Arrange

FOR THE SALSA VERDE

25 g (¾ oz) flat-leaf parsley

25 g (¾ oz) coriander
(cilantro)

75 g (2½ oz/5 tbsps) olive oil

2 tbsps lime juice, white
wine vinegar or apple
cider vinegar

½ small shallot, finely diced

½ small green chilli, finely
diced (you can leave the
seeds in if you like
something hotter)

1 anchovy fillet

SUBS

bacon – lardons or guanciale

sourdough – panko

Vin Santo – Sauternes;
sherry

white wine – chicken or
vegetable stock

green chilli – ¼ tsp chilli
(hot pepper) flakes

the carrots, leeks and celery around the base of the tray, then pour over the wine. Roast for 5–6 hours, covering the tray with foil if the meat is browning too quickly, until the internal temperature of the meat is 75°C (167°F).

Meanwhile, make the salsa verde. Place the herbs in a food processor or very finely chop by hand. Mix in the oil until smooth, then remove and place in a bowl. Stir in the rest of the ingredients and season to taste. As long as you finely chop your chilli and shallot this method works fine, but if you are in a hurry or prefer a smooth consistency by all means blitz everything in the food processor.

Once cooked, allow the meat to rest for at least 15 minutes, ideally 20–30 minutes. Serve the porchetta in slices with a good dollop of the salsa. I like to have this with the Potato and Chard Gratin on page 159 or alternatively allow to porchetta to cool down completely and refrigerate overnight. The next day, thinly slice and serve in between 2 slices of focaccia with some good mayo and lots more salsa verde.

FEASTING MENUS

CROWD PLEASER

TO EAT

Fried Olives pg. 92

Pork Shoulder with Rhubarb Ketchup
pg. 112

French Beans, Mustard and Shallots
pg. 153

Potato and Chard Gratin
pg. 159

Baked Apples and Pine Nut Crumble
pg. 196

TO DRINK

Old Fashioned
(For 1: muddle together 1 tsp demerara
sugar, 3 tbsps whisky, 4 dashes of
bitters, a strip of orange zest and some
ice. Strain into a lowball glass with
3 large ice cubes. Twist another strip
of orange zest over the glass and use
to garnish.)

ITALIAN TRATTORIA

TO EAT

Tortellini in Brodo pg. 106

Classic Shallot Dressing with
Tomatoes pg. 144

Focaccia

Puntarelle with Anchovy Dressing
pg. 149

Tiramisu pg. 187

TO DRINK

Prosecco with a dash of Fennel Syrup
(see Fennel and Ginger cocktail recipe
on pg. 81)

SUNDAY SUPPER

TO EAT

Avocado Dressing with Baby Gem
Lettuce pg. 145

Spatchcock Chicken pg. 116

Buttered Leek Croquettes pg. 100

Walnut and Caramel Tart pg. 177

TO DRINK

Fennel and Ginger pg. 81

LAZY SUPPER

TO EAT

Lamb with Aubergine pg. 114

Green Bulgur Wheat pg. 156

Miso Mayo with Asparagus
pg. 148

Buttermilk Panna Cotta with Boozy
Greengages pg. 191

TO DRINK

a good red wine

SUMMER DINNER

TO EAT

Pickled Radish, Fennel and Chicory
Salad pg. 161

Flatbread
(Mix 200 g/7 oz/1⅔ cups self-raising flour
with 200 g/7 oz/generous ¾ cup
yoghurt and season with salt and freshly
ground black pepper. Once just combined,
divide into four balls. Roll out each ball
gently on a lightly floured work surface
to 5 mm/¼ in thick. Griddle in a hot pan
on both sides until puffed up and cooked
through. Cover with a clean dish towel and
keep warm until ready to serve.)

Spiced Lamb with Hummus
pg. 104

Broccoli and Pea Salad pg. 134

Caraway and Pistachio Cake
pg. 170

Spiced Almonds pg. 94

TO DRINK

Mint Julep
(For 1: place 5 mint leaves, 3 tbsps
bourbon (I use Maker's Mark), 1 tbsp
simple syrup and 2 dashes of bitters
into a shaker with some ice. Shake well,
then strain into a glass filled with
crushed ice. Muddle together with a
few more mint leaves and serve.)

FESTIVE FEAST

TO EAT

Celeriac and Apple Soup pg. 33

Porchetta pg. 124

Bread Sauce with Sprouts
and Hazelnuts pg. 138

Sherry and Quince Trifle pg. 184

TO DRINK

Crémant served with 1 tbsp
clementine juice and a sprig
of rosemary

CHAPTER FIVE

On the *side*

Broccoli *and* Pea Salad

Serves 4

150 g (5 oz) kale, stems
　　removed, chopped
½ tsp salt, or more to taste
150 g (5 oz/1 cup) fresh
　　garden peas
300 g (10½ oz) broccoli,
　　chopped into small bite-
　　size pieces
3 tbsps olive oil
zest and juice of ½ lemon
50 g (2 oz/⅓ cup)
　　macadamia nuts
10 g (½ oz) chervil, finely
　　chopped
5 g (¼ oz) coriander
　　(cilantro), finely
　　chopped
25 g (¾ oz) pecorino, shaved
freshly ground black pepper

SUBS
kale – cavolo nero; chard
peas – broad (fava) beans
　　(blanched and peeled);
　　mangetout (snow peas)
broccoli – romanesco
macadamia – walnuts

Raw broccoli is something that is often overlooked when it comes to veg prep, but I love the crunch it adds. It is also really important to add the salt to the kale and massage it well, as this will completely transform the flavour.

Place the chopped kale in a bowl and cover with the salt. Use your hands to massage the salt into the kale to soften. It should become tender and look darker green in colour. Add the peas and mix the broccoli, then dress with the oil, lemon zest and juice and season with black pepper. Taste to see if more salt is required.

In a dry frying pan (skillet), toast the macadamia nuts before crushing in a pestle and mortar. Add to the salad along with the herbs and pecorino and toss together.

This is best eaten at room temperature within a few hours of making it.

Roasted Greens *with* Ajo Blanco

Serves 4

300 g (10½ oz) greens
  (I use a mixture of
  asparagus, French beans
  and Tenderstem broccoli,
  but you can use just one)
olive oil, for drizzling
2 tbsps capers
50 g (2 oz) butter
chervil, finely chopped, to
  garnish *(optional)*

FOR THE AJO BLANCO
125 g (4 oz) flaked (slivered)
  almonds
1 garlic clove
1 tsp sherry or white wine
  vinegar
3 tbsps olive oil
75 g (2½ oz) ice-cold water,
  more to loosen if required
salt and freshly ground
  black pepper

SUBS
flaked almonds – blanched
  hazelnuts
capers – chopped green
  olives

This is a dish that me and my friend Will made during the course of our pop-up restaurant. I would be more than happy to enjoy it as is with some bread. It is almost essential for soaking up all of that lovely caper-y butter.

Preheat the oven to 220°C fan (475°F/gas 9).

Prep your greens so they are all similar sizes and thicknesses. For example, if using French beans and asparagus, slice your Tenderstem broccoli lengthways so it is a similar thickness and will therefore cook in a similar period of time. Coat your greens in a little olive oil and season lightly. Toss together to coat and then place on a baking tray (pan).

For the ajo blanco, scatter the almonds over a separate baking tray and place in the oven for 2 minutes or until they are very pale golden and fragrant. You aren't looking for as much colour on these as you normally would. Weigh out 100 g (3½ oz) of the almonds and place in a food processor. (If you like you can place the remaining almonds back in the oven for a minute to get a little more colour.) Add the garlic, vinegar, oil and a little seasoning and blitz on a high speed until smooth, about 2 minutes. With the motor still running, pour in the water. Continue to blitz until silky. Check the seasoning and adjust accordingly. This can be stored in the refrigerator for up to 3 days, so can be made ahead of time.

Roast the greens in the oven for 5 minutes. Be careful not to overcook them as you want them to keep a bit of their bite.

Just before serving, heat a medium frying pan (skillet) with a little oil over a high heat. Add the capers and fry until crispy and 'popping'. Add the butter and then remove from the heat when beginning to foam.

To assemble the dish, spoon the ajo blanco onto a platter. Arrange the greens over the top, then spoon the butter and crispy capers all over the dish. Garnish with the extra toasted almonds, a good crack of black pepper and some finely chopped chervil (if using).

Bread Sauce *with* Sprouts *and* Hazelnuts

Serves 4

FOR THE BREAD SAUCE
550 g (19 fl oz/2 generous
    cups) milk
100 g (3½ oz/scant ½ cup)
    double (heavy) cream
50 g (2 oz) butter
1 bay leaf
5 cloves
1 banana shallot, halved
5 black peppercorns
nutmeg, for grating
100 g (3½ oz/1¼ cups)
    breadcrumbs
salt and freshly ground
    black pepper

FOR THE SPROUTS AND
    HAZELNUTS
olive oil, for cooking
175 g (6 oz) sprouts, halved
5 g (¼ oz) sage, finely
    chopped
30 g (1 oz/¼ cup) hazelnuts,
    roughly chopped
50 g (2 oz) butter
salt and freshly ground
    black pepper

SUBS
cream – more milk
shallot – a small white onion
hazelnuts – chestnuts

Sprouts (and bread sauce) are not just for Christmas. They are delicious finely sliced in a slaw, but fried like this is my favourite way to prepare them. Make sure you don't overcook them, as the crunchier the better.

Place your milk, cream and butter in a medium saucepan. Add the bay leaf, cloves, shallot and peppercorns. Grate in a little nutmeg. Bring to the boil and simmer for 5 minutes. Remove from the heat and allow to infuse for a minimum of 30 minutes, ideally 1 hour.

When infused, strain the milk and return it to the pan. Add the breadcrumbs and cook over a medium heat until it begins to thicken. Whisk regularly to stop it from sticking. Remove from the heat when it is just a little looser than you would like. Season to taste.

Heat a frying pan (skillet) with a little olive oil over a high heat. Add the sprouts, cut-sides down, and cook for a minute, or until coloured but still crunchy. Add the sage and hazelnuts to the pan along with the butter and cook for a further minute. Remove from the heat and season to taste.

If the bread sauce has thickened too much while you were cooking the sprouts, simply add in a splash of cream and stir over a low heat to loosen. Pour into a shallow bowl, spoon the sprouts on top and drizzle with the melted butter.

SUPPER

Squash *and* Sage Flatbreads

Makes 2 large flatbreads to
serve 4 people

125 g (4 oz/½ cup) water

75 g (2½ oz) active
sourdough starter (see
note on page 142)

195 g (7 oz/1⅔ cups) strong
white bread flour (or extra
strong if you can get hold
of it), plus extra for dusting

5 g (¼ oz) salt

olive oil, for greasing and
drizzling

400 g (14 oz) squash, peeled
(I love delicata)

5 g (¼ oz) sage, plus extra
to garnish, picked

2 rosemary sprigs, picked

¼ tsp chilli (hot pepper)
flakes

fine semolina, for dusting

100 g (3½ oz) gorgonzola

20 g (¾ oz) Parmesan

50 g (2 oz/3 tbsps) crème
fraîche

salt and freshly ground
black pepper

These are brilliant as a starter, side dish and as a
midweek dinner, so I was at a loss as to where to put
them in this book. When we are feasting, however, I like
to serve these as a side dish with many other salads and
veg platters.

The day before cooking, place the water, starter, flour and
salt in the bowl of a freestanding mixer fitted with a dough
hook and mix on a medium speed for 10 minutes. The dough
should be silky and elastic. You can knead by hand but this
will take approximately 20 minutes. Place in a lightly oiled
bowl, cover and store in the refrigerator for at least 24 hours,
or up to 48 hours.

If you want to roast your squash in advance too, preheat the
oven to 200°C (400°F/gas 6).

Scoop the inside of the squash out and place in a colander.
Wash off any excess flesh from the seeds and place them on
a clean dish towel to dry off. Cut the squash into quarters,
then into 1 cm (½ in) slices. Place on a baking tray (pan) and
drizzle with olive oil. Season well, then add the sage and
rosemary. Sprinkle over the chilli flakes. Roast for 15–25
minutes, or until the squash is soft and beginning to colour.
Allow to cool and store in a tub in the refrigerator until ready
to cook.

Pat the squash seeds with the dish towel to make sure they
are really dry, then add to another baking tray. Drizzle with
oil and season well. Bake for 5 minutes, then remove from
the oven and stir well. Put back into the oven for another few
minutes and repeat this process until they are fully dried out,
crisp and golden. Allow to cool down before storing in an
airtight container until ready to serve.

When ready to cook, place a heavy-based ovenproof pan (ideally cast-iron) over a high heat. Preheat your grill (broiler) to its highest setting.

Remove the dough from the refrigerator and tip onto a surface dusted with fine semolina. Cut into two equal pieces and dust with a little flour. Dust your hands with a little flour and pull out each piece of dough to form a round that is roughly the same size as your pan. Don't be tempted to use a rolling pin as it will knock out the air. You should find the dough stretches and presses into shape fairly easily, but if it is resisting a little simply place to one side, cover with a dish towel, and leave for 5 minutes to allow the dough to relax. They key here is not to over-handle.

When the pan is very hot, move the first piece of dough into the pan. It should start puffing up and forming bubbles. Working quickly, place half of the squash over the top. Crumble over half of the gorgonzola, finely grate half of the Parmesan over and spoon dollops of half of the crème fraîche on top. Finish with a few sage leaves, a crack of black pepper and a good drizzle of oil. Place the pan under the grill (broiler) immediately and cook for 2–3 minutes, keeping a careful eye so it doesn't burn. Turn if colouring unevenly. Once you have some blackened blisters and the cheese has melted and is bubbling nicely, it is ready. Remove from the pan and set aside on a board.

Repeat this process with the second piece of dough (please be careful with the hot pan).

When ready to serve, cut the flatbreads in half and sprinkle with the roasted squash seeds.

NOTE

If you don't have an active starter, simply use 36 g (1¼ oz/ generous ¼ cup) flour, 36 g (1¼ oz/2 tbsps plus 1 tsp) water and ½ tsp instant yeast in its place.

Roasted New Potatoes
with 'Nduja Butter

Serves 4 as a side

3 tbsps goose fat

1.2 kg (1 lb 5 oz) new potatoes

3 rosemary sprigs

6 garlic cloves, unpeeled

75 g (2½ oz) unsalted
    butter

75 g (2½ oz) 'nduja

2 tsps white wine vinegar

75 g (2½ oz/5 tbsps) olive oil

salt and freshly ground
    black pepper

dill fronds, to serve

SUBS

goose fat – olive oil

rosemary – sage

white wine vinegar – lemon
    juice

'Nduja is a like a soft salami with a good bit of heat to it. It's delicious when stirred through most dishes, but I particularly like to use it in the winter months, when the kick of heat that runs through it will really do the job of warming me up.

Preheat the oven to 200°C fan (430°F/gas 8).

Place a roasting tray (pan) in the oven with the goose fat for 5 minutes or until it is shimmering. Carefully add the potatoes, shake the pan the coat them in the fat and return to the oven for 20 minutes.

Strip the rosemary sprigs but keep the stalk. Remove the roasting tray from the oven and add the garlic cloves and rosemary, stalk and all. Season lightly with salt and return to the oven for another 20 minutes or until golden and crispy. Make sure the garlic doesn't burn – you can remove it early if it is.

When nearly ready, add the butter, 'nduja, vinegar and oil into the bowl of a food processor. Squeeze the roasted garlic out of its skin and add to the processor. Blitz on a high speed until smooth and creamy. Season to taste.

Serve the potatoes either in a bowl with the butter on the side, or on a platter with the butter spooned over while the potatoes are still warm to allow it to melt. Garnish with a few dill fronds.

DRESSINGS FOR SALADS
AND VEGETABLES

TURMERIC AND TAHINI DRESSING WITH POTATOES

Serves 2

1 tsp ground turmeric
a small piece of fresh ginger
1 small garlic clove
1 tbsp tahini
1 tbsp honey
juice of ½ lemon
3 tbsps olive oil, or as needed
salt and freshly ground black pepper

TO SERVE
300 g (10½ oz) baby potatoes,
    boiled

SUBS
potatoes – roasted sweet potato;
    roasted carrots

Place all the ingredients into the small bowl of a food processor and blitz until smooth and creamy. If too thick, you can loosen with either more oil or a little water. Season to taste.

Store in a glass jar in the refrigerator for up to 3 days. Toss through some boiled baby potatoes to serve.

CLASSIC SHALLOT DRESSING WITH TOMATOES

Serve 4–6

1 small banana shallot
2 tsps white wine vinegar
1 tsp honey
1 tsp Dijon mustard
3 tbsps olive oil
salt and freshly ground black pepper

TO SERVE
300 g (10½ oz) heritage tomatoes
10 g (½ oz) fresh oregano

SUBS
tomatoes – asparagus; baby gem lettuce

Finely chop the shallots. Whisk together in a bowl with the vinegar, honey and mustard until smooth. Slowly add the oil while whisking to combine. Season to taste.

Slice the tomatoes and arrange on a platter. Spoon over the dressing and garnish with the oregano leaves.

AVOCADO DRESSING WITH BABY GEM LETTUCE

Serves 2

1 avocado
1 garlic clove
40 g (1½ oz/scant 3 tbsps) lemon juice
25 g (¾ oz) herbs: basil, parsley, coriander/
    cilantro, chives (use any mixture that
    suits what you have)
a small piece of fresh ginger, grated
40 g (1½ oz/scant 3 tbsps) olive oil
40 g (1½ oz/scant 3 tbsps) water
10 g (½ oz) tahini
¼ tsp chilli (hot pepper) flakes
salt and freshly ground black pepper

TO SERVE
1–2 baby gem lettuces
sesame seeds, toasted

SUBS
baby gem – iceberg, cut into wedges;
    mizuna; rocket (arugula); oak leaf lettuce

Place all the ingredients in a food processor and blitz until smooth. Season to taste.

Serve with baby gem lettuce and a sprinkle of sesame seeds.

CHILLI AND CUCUMBER SALAD

Serves 2

3 tbsps white wine vinegar
30 g (1 oz/2 tbsps) caster (superfine) sugar
½ red onion, finely sliced
thumb-sized piece of fresh ginger, peeled
    and finely sliced
2 tbsps sesame oil
1 cucumber
10 g (½ oz) mint leaves, finely sliced
1 small red chilli, deseeded and finely sliced
1 tbsp poppy seeds
salt and freshly ground black pepper

SUBS
cucumber – carrot ribbons; courgette (zucchini)
    ribbons; chicory (endive) leaves

Bring the vinegar and sugar to the boil in a small saucepan until the sugar has dissolved. Stir in the sliced onion and remove from the heat. Add the ginger to the pan with a little salt, then stir in the sesame oil.

Cut the cucumber in half lengthways, scoop out and discard the seeds, then cut at an angle into 2 cm (¾ in) slices. Place in a bowl. Add the mint, chilli and poppy seeds along with the dressing. Toss to combine, then season to taste.

Serve immediately.

MISO MAYO WITH ASPARAGUS

Serves 2

1 egg
1 tbsp white miso
1 tsp grainy mustard
juice of ½ lemon (zest first and reserve
    some for garnishing)
100 g (3½ oz/scant ½ cup) sunflower oil
salt and freshly ground black pepper

TO SERVE
250 g (9 oz) asparagus, chervil blanched
    or dill

SUBS
asparagus – French beans;
    Tenderstem broccoli

Place all the ingredients, except the oil,
in the small bowl of a food processor
and blitz on a high speed until combined.
With the motor still running, slowly pour
in the oil in a trickle until a thick mayo
has formed. Season to taste.

Serve spooned over some blanched
asparagus and garnish with the lemon
zest and herbs.

LIME AND GINGER DRESSING WITH CARROTS AND PEANUTS

Serves 2

juice of 1 lime
½ small green chilli, deseeded
1 tsp soy sauce
1 tsp white wine vinegar
1 tsp honey
small piece of fresh ginger
1 garlic clove
about 4 tbsps sesame oil
salt and freshly ground black pepper

TO SERVE
2 carrots
1 spring onion (scallion)
50 g (2 oz/⅓ cup) salted peanuts
1 tbsp black sesame seeds

SUBS
carrots – cucumber; sugar snap peas

Place all the ingredients for the dressing,
except the oil and seasoning, in the small
bowl of a food processor. Blitz on a high
speed until smooth and well combined.
Add the oil and blitz again. You may require
more oil depending on the strength of
your chilli and ginger. Season to taste.

Peel the carrots and then continue to
peel into ribbons. Finely slice the spring
onions lengthways into 5 cm (2 in) strips.
Coarsely chop the peanuts and mix with
the carrots and onions in a serving bowl.
Add the sesame seeds. Finally add the
dressing, to taste.

PUNTARELLE WITH ANCHOVY DRESSING

If you are struggling to find puntarelle you can always use some regular chicory leaves instead.

Serves 2–4

1 small puntarelle
2 anchovy fillets
1 small garlic clove
4 tbsps extra virgin olive oil
1 tbsp white wine vinegar
a small pinch of chilli (hot pepper) flakes
    (optional)
pecorino, for grating
freshly ground black pepper

SUBS
puntarelle – chicory (endive);
   radicchio; fennel

To prepare the puntarelle, break off the outer leaves (use them in a stir-fry later). Once you can see the pale core, clip off the hollow stems. You may need a knife as you work your way towards the centre. Slice each of the stems into matchsticks and place in a large bowl of iced water. Set aside for 2 hours or until the puntarelle has curled.

For the dressing, mash together the anchovies and garlic with a little pepper to form a paste. Add the oil and vinegar and mix well. Add the chilli, if using.

Drain the puntarelle and dry well. Toss with the dressing, then serve on a plate with a generous grating of pecorino.

Runner Beans *with* Mint *and* Tomatoes

Serves 4 as a side

olive oil, for cooking

4 banana shallots, finely
   sliced

1 courgette (zucchini), finely
   sliced

4 garlic cloves, finely sliced

1–2 anchovy fillets

200 g (7 oz) cherry tomatoes

100 g (3½ oz/scant ½ cup)
   white wine

100 g (3½ oz/scant ½ cup)
   water or vegetable stock

150 g (5 oz) stringless runner
   beans

25 g (¾ oz) mint, leaves
   roughly chopped

salt and freshly ground
   black pepper

SUBS

shallots – red onion

anchovies – 1 tsp capers

white wine – chicken or veg
   stock

runner beans – French
   beans; broad (fava) beans
   (shells removed)

Runner beans are not my go-to green, but after a glut from our local growers required some imagination, I taught myself to adore them. This recipe is based on a delicious meal I had at the Kinneuchar Inn a few years ago. The use of mint was inspired and I knew I wanted to try to recreate it.

Heat a little olive oil in a medium saucepan that has a lid over a medium heat. Add the shallots and cook until softened and golden, then add the courgette and garlic, season and cover with the lid. Cook for 5–10 minutes, stirring occasionally, until completely softened. Add the anchovy (add two if you like a stronger flavour) and the tomatoes, then pour in the wine and cover again. Cook for a further 10 minutes (turn down the heat to a simmer if required). Keep stirring occasionally to stop anything sticking. The tomatoes should break down entirely once they have softened.

Cut the beans diagonally into 3 cm (1 in) chunks. Add the beans and mint to the pan with a splash more water if the sauce has thickened too much. Cook for 2 minutes, then remove from the heat and serve. Delicious with lamb (place any roasting juices in with the sauce) and a good dollop of aioli.

French Beans, Mustard
and Shallots

Serves 2–4 as a side

20 g (¾ oz/2½ tbsps)
pumpkin seeds
a small knob of butter
a drizzle of olive oil
2 banana shallots (medium-
sized), finely sliced
lengthways
75 g (2½ oz/5 tbsps) white
wine
150 g (5 oz) French beans
100 g (3½ oz) peas (frozen
or fresh)
1 tarragon sprig, leaves
finely chopped
10 g (½ oz) flat-leaf parsley,
finely chopped
75 g (2½ oz) crème fraîche
1 tsp Dijon mustard
10 g (½ oz) chives, finely
chopped, or more parsley
salt and freshly ground
black pepper

SUBS
pumpkin seeds – sunflower
seeds; flaked (slivered)
almonds
shallots – red onion; spring
onions (scallions)
white wine – veg stock
crème fraîche – sour cream
peas – broad (fava) beans

A simple way to dress up your beans and greens.

In a medium frying pan (skillet) over a medium-high heat,
toast the pumpkin seeds until beginning to colour and pop.
Set aside in a bowl.

Heat a little butter and olive oil in the same pan over a
medium heat, add the shallots and cook until softened and
beginning to colour. Add the wine and cook for 1 minute,
then add the beans and peas. Cook for 2 minutes, or until
just cooked, the French beans still being quite al dente.
Stir in the tarragon and parsley and remove from the heat.

Whisk together the crème fraîche and mustard in a bowl
and add to the pan. Mix well. Season to taste.

Serve warm on a platter, scattered with the toasted pumpkin
seeds and the chives or more parsley if you prefer.

Roasted Peppers
with Anchovy Sauce

Serves 4–6 as a side

2 ramiro/romano (sweet
   pointed) peppers
25 g (¾ oz) anchovy fillets
1 garlic clove, minced
2 tsps white wine vinegar
2 egg yolks
75 g (2½ oz/5 tbsps)
   sunflower oil
100 g (3½ oz) mixed cherry
   tomatoes
10 g (½ oz) flat-leaf parsley
10 g (½ oz) chervil
small handful of watercress
extra virgin olive oil, for
   drizzling
sumac or chilli (hot pepper)
   flakes, depending on how
   you like your spice
salt and freshly ground
   black pepper

SUBS
egg yolks – 1 whole egg
cherry tomatoes – plum or
   heritage tomatoes, sliced
chervil – more parsley

This is very similar to a tonnato sauce, but with anchovies instead of tuna for the base. Use roasted red peppers from a jar as a speedy alternative here. Standard bell peppers will work well too, but the sweeter variety ramiro is a much better match for the anchovies.

Char the peppers whole over a flame for 5 minutes, or until blackened and softening slightly. Alternatively, you can place underneath a hot grill (broiler) and move every minute or so to colour evenly – again, you are looking for blackened blisters on the skin. Once cooked, place in a heatproof bowl, cover and set aside.

To make the anchovy sauce, blitz together the anchovies, garlic, vinegar and egg yolks in the small bowl of a food processor until combined. With the motor still running, slowly trickle in the oil as you would for a mayonnaise or aioli. Once all of the oil has been added, you should have a thick sauce. Season to taste (you should only really need a little pepper for this, as the saltiness come from the anchovies). Spread the sauce over your plates.

Remove the peppers from the bowl and use a knife or your hands to peel away the skins. Don't worry if you have a little black left on the pepper as this helps with the flavour. Cut the skinned peppers in half and scrape out the seeds, then slice into long strips. Arrange the strips folded and draped over the anchovy sauce. Cut the cherry tomatoes in half and arrange over the peppers, then pick the parsley and chervil leaves and scatter over the top with a little watercress. Drizzle with some extra virgin olive oil, and garnish with some sumac or chilli flakes, depending on your preference.

Green Bulgur Wheat

Serves 4–6 as a side

50 g (2 oz/generous ½ cup) flaked (slivered) almonds
200 g (7 oz) bulgur wheat
700 g (1 lb 9 oz/scant 3 cups) vegetable stock
150 g (5 oz) spinach
25 g (¾ oz) basil
25 g (¾ oz) coriander (cilantro), plus extra to serve
10 g (½ oz) dill
100 g (3½ oz/scant ½ cup) extra virgin olive oil, plus extra to serve
3 tbsps rapeseed (canola) oil
2 garlic cloves
juice of 1 lime
½ tsp Aleppo pepper
salt
75 g (2½ oz) feta cheese, to garnish

SUBS
bulgur wheat – pasta; pearl couscous; beans
spinach – more basil, parsley or coriander – you need about 200 g (7 oz) total weight of herbs
rapeseed oil – more olive oil
almonds – pine nuts

This recipe is a riff on the classic pesto pasta and is a result of me craving said dish only to discover we had no pasta, no Parmesan and hardly any basil. Probably enough to make anyone abort the plan, but alas I am stubborn and this was the result.

Toast the almonds in a dry pan until fragrant and golden. Set aside to cool down.

Bring the bulgur wheat and vegetable stock to the boil in a large saucepan. Cook for 5–10 minutes, or as instructed on the packet. Once cooked, the bulgur wheat should still have a bit of a bite to it. Drain and set aside, making sure you keep it warm.

Place the spinach, basil, coriander and dill in a food processor and blitz. Season with a little salt and continue to blitz until the greens are smooth and well combined. You may need to scrape down the sides of the processor regularly for this. Add the oils, garlic and toasted almonds and blitz again until smooth. Lastly, add the lime juice and the Aleppo pepper. Season once more to taste, then stir the green sauce through the warm bulgur wheat.

Serve warm with a little bit of crumbled feta, coriander leaves and extra virgin olive oil drizzled on the top. Alternatively, you can allow this to cool down completely and serve as a salad with a little bit more oil and some greens mixed through it.

Cheesy Polenta

Serves 4 as a side

200 g (7 oz/1⅓ cups)
   polenta
1 kg (2 lb 4 oz/4 cups) boiling
   water, plus extra to
   loosen
1 Parmesan rind
50 g (2 oz) butter
40 g (1½ oz) Cheddar,
   grated
40 g (1½ oz) Parmesan,
   grated
40 g (1½ oz) Gruyère, grated
salt and freshly ground
   black pepper

The volume of dairy in this recipe will either entice you or terrify you. Either way, it is worth cooking and serving with a pile of rich tomato meatballs. You can even finish it with more cheese on top, if you are feeling particularly hardcore.

Place the polenta and water in a large saucepan with a pinch of salt. Whisk together continuously over a medium heat for 5–10 minutes until thickened and smooth. You can use a wooden spoon for this, but I find a whisk works best. Add more water if the mix becomes too stodgy. Keep whisking for another 10 minutes until the polenta is silky and smooth. Reduce the heat if it is catching. This process reminds me of a cross between constantly stirring risottos and beating eggs into choux pastry – it's labour intensive, but the result is noticeable when it comes to the finished texture. After the polenta has been cooking for 20 minutes and is no longer gritty, whisk in the butter. Add all of the cheeses to the pan, whisking regularly. Season with pepper to taste (there should be enough saltiness from the cheese), then serve immediately.

Potato *and* Chard Gratin

Serves 4–6 as a side

1 kg (2 lb 4 oz) potatoes,
    skin on
250 g (9 oz) chard
250 g (9 oz) double (heavy)
    cream
1 tsp salt
1 tsp freshly ground black
    pepper
4 garlic cloves, minced
100 g (3½ oz) Parmesan,
    finely grated
small bunch of sage,
    finely chopped
small bunch of marjoram
    leaves, finely chopped
50 g (2 oz) butter

SUBS
chard – collard greens;
    spinach; kale
Parmesan – Gruyère; Grana
    Padano
sage – rosemary; thyme;
    marjoram

Potatoes, cream, garlic. What could possibly be better?

Preheat the oven to 190°C fan (410°F/gas 7).

Using a mandoline, food processor or very sharp knife, finely slice the potatoes into discs about 3 mm (⅛ in) thick. Strip the leaves from the stems of the chard and chop the leaves roughly. Finely slice the stems. Set aside.

In a bowl, mix together the cream, seasoning, garlic, half of the Parmesan and all of the chopped herbs. Whisk well, then mix in the potato slices and chard leaves, ensuring everything is evenly coated.

Place the chard stems in the bottom of an ovenproof dish (ideally one with a lid – I like to use a round, shallow, 23 cm/ 9 in cast-iron dish). Pour the creamy potato and chard mixture on top and sprinkle the remaining Parmesan over. Slice the butter into slivers and arrange over the top. Cover with the lid or some foil and bake for 50 minutes, removing the lid after 25 minutes, until a knife comes out of the centre easily and the potatoes are cooked through.

Enjoy immediately. This dish can be made ahead of time, refrigerated, then cooked just before serving, however I wouldn't recommend keeping it in the refrigerator for any longer than 6 hours in case the potatoes begin to discolour.

Pickled Radish, Fennel *and* Chicory Salad

Serves 4–6 as a side

FOR THE PICKLED RADISH
250 g (9 oz) radishes
125 g (4 oz/½ cup) white
   wine vinegar
75 g (2½ oz/5 tbsps) water
50 g (2 oz/¼ cup) caster
   (superfine) sugar
1 tsp salt

FOR THE SALAD
1 fennel bulb
2 heads of chicory (endive)
250 g (9 oz) mixed colour
   radishes
10 g (½ oz) fennel fronds
   or dill
20 g (¾ oz/3 tbsps)
   sunflower seeds
extra virgin olive oil, to taste
lemon juice, to taste
handful of fresh rose petals
   (optional)
salt and freshly ground
   black pepper

SUBS
chicory – radicchio
sunflower seeds – pumpkin
   seeds
fennel fronds – dill

A light, bright, zingy salad that is perfect for a light meal or a colourful feast of an evening.

Begin by making the pickled radish. Using a mandoline or a food processor, finely slice the radishes into 1–2 mm (¹⁄₁₆ in) discs. Set aside in a heatproof bowl.

Weigh out the vinegar, water, sugar and salt into a saucepan and bring to the boil until the sugar is fully dissolved. Pour the mixture over the radish slices and set aside to cool. Store in an airtight container in the refrigerator for up to 2 weeks.

When ready to assemble the salad, cut the fennel into thin slices lengthways. Remove any limp outer leaves of the chicory and pick the rest of the leaves. Place in a large mixing bowl alongside the fennel. Finely slice the radishes as you did for the pickled radish and add to the bowl. Roughly chop the fennel fronds (or the dill) and add to the vegetables.

In a small frying pan (skillet), toast the sunflower seeds over a high heat until they are well coloured and starting to pop. Allow to cool.

Measure out a couple of tbsps of the pickling liquid from the radishes and add to a small bowl. Top up with extra virgin olive oil, salt and pepper to form a quick dressing. Taste as you go along. At this stage, you can add a little lemon juice or more oil if required.

To assemble, drain the radishes, reserving the pickling juice for other dressings or adding a little more to this salad. Toss the drained radishes through the leaves and the fennel and add the quick dressing. Finish with the sunflower seeds and rose petals, if using. Toss together one last time before spooning onto a large serving platter. Serve immediately.

CHAPTER SIX

Sweet endings

Spelt *and* Hazelnut Cake *with* Chocolate Sauce

Serves 8

200 g (7 oz) unsalted butter, softened, plus extra for greasing
200 g (7 oz/1 generous cup) light brown sugar
125 g (4 oz/scant 1 cup) hazelnuts
100 g (3½ oz/⅔ cup) wholemeal spelt flour
1 tsp baking powder
¼ tsp salt
4 eggs
demerara sugar, for sprinkling

FOR THE CHOCOLATE SAUCE
150 g (5 oz/scant ⅔ cup) double (heavy) cream
1 tsp vanilla bean paste
¼ tsp salt
100 g (3½ oz) chocolate, chopped (I like to use one with 50–60% cocoa solids so it isn't too bitter)
45 g (1¾ oz/2 tbsps) golden syrup

TO SERVE
crème fraîche
extra toasted chopped hazelnuts *(optional)*

Swapping out some of the flour weight for ground nuts in a cake batter has always been the fastest route to a soft cake with a tender crumb. It instantly transforms a sponge, and not only will it help keep the cake soft and moist for longer, it also makes it altogether more sophisticated, in my opinion.

Preheat the oven to 170°C fan (375°F/gas 5). Grease and line a loose-bottomed 20 cm (8 in) cake tin (pan).

In a freestanding mixer, fitted with the paddle attachment, beat together the butter and light brown sugar until light and fluffy. You can also do this by hand or with a hand-held mixer.

Place the hazelnuts on a small roasting tray (pan) and toast in the oven for 5–10 minutes until golden and fragrant. Weigh out 100 g (3½ oz) of the toasted hazelnuts and blitz in a food processor to a fine crumb. Chop up the remaining hazelnuts roughly and set aside for topping.

Add the blitzed hazelnuts to the creamed butter and sugar along with the wholemeal spelt flour, baking powder, salt and eggs. Beat again until well combined.

Spoon the mixture into the prepared cake tin and level with the back of a palette knife. Sprinkle over a generous amount of demerara sugar along with the reserved chopped hazelnuts. Bake in the oven for 40–45 minutes, or until a knife inserted into the centre of the cake comes out clean. Allow to cool down a little.

To make the chocolate sauce, heat the cream, vanilla and salt in a small saucepan until just simmering. Pour into a

SUBS

light brown sugar – half
  caster (superfine) sugar,
  half dark muscovado
wholemeal spelt –
  wholemeal flour; plain
  (all-purpose) flour; white
  spelt flour
hazelnuts – almonds, pine
  nuts
golden syrup – honey; agave

bowl and add the chopped chocolate and golden syrup. Allow to stand for a few minutes before whisking to combine. Continue to mix until thick and glossy. Serve immediately or store in the refrigerator for up to 1 week. To serve from cold, melt very gently in a bain marie so as not to burn the chocolate. Once thick and pourable, you are ready to go.

Serve the warm cake with a dollop of crème fraîche on the side and pour over the chocolate sauce. If you want, you can also add some extra toasted chopped hazelnuts on top.

The cake will keep in an airtight container for up to 3 days.

SUPPER

NO-PUDDING PUDDINGS

WHISKY ICE CREAM

Whip 200 g (7 oz/scant 1 cup) double (heavy) cream until thickened. Fold in 150 g (5 oz/scant ⅔ cup) condensed milk, ½ tsp vanilla bean paste, a small pinch of salt and 1–2 tbsps of your preferred whisky (taste while adding to achieve the strength you are after). Spoon into an airtight container and freeze. If you want to jazz it up a bit, you can layer the whipped cream mixture with some caramel sauce and chopped roasted almonds, then swirl it through the ice cream before freezing.

BERRIES AND MINT

In a pestle and mortar, bash together some caster (superfine) sugar and mint leaves to form a soft, pale green sugar. Mix through some berries to taste and allow to macerate for 10 minutes before serving. You should have deliciously fresh and sweet fruit in a syrup created by the macerating.

GINGER MERINGUE PARFAIT

Whip together 280 g (10 oz/generous 1 cup) double (heavy) cream, ½ tsp vanilla bean paste and swirl through 4 tbsps coffee liqueur. Finely slice 2 balls of stem ginger and add to the cream. Crumble in 2 large meringues (or 4 small ones) and 2 tbsps of stem ginger syrup. Fold together, then scoop into a lined loaf tin (pan). Cover and pop in the freezer for at least 2 hours. Serve from frozen in slices with a chocolate sauce spiked with coffee.

STONE FRUIT

This is the simplest after-dinner sweet hit, but only when the fruits are at their best. Soft and sweet room-temperature doughnut peaches, served with a glass of well-chilled prosecco, is bliss in one of its simplest forms. When nectarines, plums, apricots, greengages and peaches are at their finest, it is best just to serve them straight up. Crumbles, roasted fruits, jams and Bellinis are all the better when created after you have enjoyed the first of the crop in their prime.

QUICK CHOCOLATE MOUSSE

Surely this has to be one of Nigella's classic recipes. I remember making this when I was quite young with a friend and was genuinely amazed that our childish marshmallows could make something so grown-up-looking. It's the only reason I ever have marshmallows in the house and is an excellent fall-back plan when you need something chocolatey. I have tweaked Nigella's version slightly, but the satisfaction is still the same! Melt 75 g (2½ oz) mini marshmallows with 25 g (¾ oz) butter, 100 g (3½ oz) chopped, dark chocolate and 25 g (¾ oz/scant 2 tbsps) water. Whip 100 g (3½ oz/scant ½ cup) double (heavy) cream with a little vanilla bean paste until thick, then fold in the chocolate mixture. Spoon between espresso cups or old-fashioned champagne flutes and chill for 5 minutes, or longer if required. Serve with some shaved chocolate, if you have the time or inclination.

SILKY CUSTARD

Heat 140 g (4½ oz/generous ½ cup) double (heavy) cream in a pan with 100 g (3½ oz/scant ½ cup) milk and 1 tsp vanilla bean paste. In a bowl, whisk together 2 heaped tsps cornflour (cornstarch), 1 egg and 60 g (2¼ oz/¼ cup) caster (superfine) sugar. Pour the hot cream over the top of the egg mixture and whisk together. Return to the pan and cook over a medium-low heat, whisking continuously, until it reaches 82°C (180°F). Serve with a slice of pandoro, a warm sponge cake, a scoop of crumble or simply on its own in a wee ramekin with toasted almonds and amaretti biscuits crushed over the top.

FIGS WITH HONEY AND MASCARPONE

Whisk some honey and mascarpone together with a little vanilla bean paste. Taste for sweetness and adjust accordingly. Heat 1 part water and 1 part caster (superfine) sugar in a pan. Bring to the boil until dissolved, then add a halved fig per person, a tsp of amaretto per person and a thyme sprig. Cook for 1 minute until the figs are just softening. Remove from the heat and stir in a little more honey to taste. Spoon the mascarpone mixture into glasses or small cups, then top each with a warm fig and some syrup.

AFFOGATO

It's uncomplicated and delicious. The best one I have had was made with Vanilla and Mascarpone Gelato (from our friend Joe Sykes of Joelato) and since then it has been unbeaten. A double shot of espresso poured over any ice cream you want and served immediately. I like to sprinkle crushed amaretti biscuits on the top, too. Truly one of my desert island puds.

Caraway *and* Pistachio Cake

Serves 8

150 g (5 oz/1 cup) pistachios
1 tsp caraway seeds
100 g (3½ oz/1 cup) ground
 almonds (almond meal)
1 tsp baking powder
75 g (2½ oz) unsalted butter
75 g (2½ oz/5 tbsps) light-
 tasting extra virgin olive
 oil (see intro)
3 eggs
200 g (7 oz/generous 1 cup)
 light brown sugar
½ tsp vanilla bean paste
¼ tsp salt

TO SERVE
crème fraîche
honey

SUBS
pistachios – for a cheaper
 cake, swap half of the
 weight with more almonds
 or some hazelnuts
light brown sugar – caster
 (superfine) sugar

The first time I made this cake, it worked perfectly. However, the fruitier extra virgin olive oil I used the second time around changed it drastically. Make sure you sample the oil you plan to use first and choose a delicate one.

Preheat the oven to 170°C fan (375°F/gas 5). Grease and line a loose-bottomed 20 cm (8 in) cake tin (pan).

Blitz the pistachios with the caraway seeds in a food processor until finely ground. Place in a large bowl and whisk in the almonds and baking powder until evenly combined.

Melt the butter gently over a low heat. Once melted, stir in the olive oil and set aside to cool.

Whisk together the eggs, sugar, vanilla and salt in a freestanding mixer fitted with the whisk attachment until pale, light and fluffy (this should take 2–3 minutes of mixing on a high speed). You can also do this with an electric hand mixer.

To make the batter, pour half of the butter and oil mix over the nuts and whisk to combine. Next, add half of the pale egg mixture and fold gently until evenly mixed. Pour the final half of the butter into the bowl and fold again, being careful not to knock out any air. Lastly, pour the rest of the egg mix into the bowl and gently fold again. Carefully pour into your tin.

Bake for 45–55 minutes, or until golden and risen. The middle will still be slightly soft (a knife won't come out of the centre clean) but if it still has quite a wobble to it, cook for a further 5–10 minutes. Remove from the oven and allow to cool.

The cake will sink in the middle, but don't worry. Serve with a good dollop of crème fraîche and some honey.

Milk Ice Cream *with* Black Pepper Strawberries

Serves 4 (with leftovers)

FOR THE MILK ICE CREAM
350 g (12 oz/generous
  1⅓ cups) whole (full-fat)
  milk
100 g (3½ oz/scant ½ cup)
  double (heavy) cream
3 egg yolks
40 g (1½ oz/3 tbsps) caster
  (superfine) sugar
10 g (½ oz/2 tbsps) dried
  milk powder
rose petals, to garnish

FOR THE BLACK PEPPER
  STRAWBERRIES
250 g (9 oz) strawberries,
  chopped or halved,
  depending on size
25 g (¾ oz/2 tbsps) caster
  (superfine) sugar
½ tsp freshly ground black
  pepper, plus extra to
  serve

SUBS
strawberries – nectarines
whole milk – 250 g (9 oz/
  1 cup) semi-skimmed
  (half-fat) milk mixed with
  100 g (3½ oz/scant ½ cup)
  additional cream (boil
  together and reduce as
  described in the method)

I almost never work with milk powder, but here I do feel it brings a welcome and almost malty flavour to the ice cream. As someone once said to me when commenting on a fairly hipster restaurant menu, 'Surely all ice cream is milk ice cream?'. They are not wrong, but I do feel like this one deserves the title.

Bring the milk to a simmer over a medium heat in a saucepan and continue to cook until the milk has reduced by nearly half. Stir in the cream while still on the heat.

In a bowl, whisk together the egg yolks, sugar and milk powder. Pour the hot milk mixture over the yolks and whisk together.

Return the mixture to the saucepan over a medium-low heat and heat until it reaches 82°C (180°F), or until it coats the back of a wooden spoon, whisking and mixing all the time so that it doesn't curdle or split at the bottom.

Remove from the heat and use a hand-held blender to blitz until emulsified. Set aside to cool completely. You can do this in a bowl placed in a sink full of ice or in the refrigerator.

Once chilled, churn in your ice-cream maker following the manufacturer's instructions. Store in the freezer until ready to serve (it will store well for up to 2 months).

Just before serving, make the black pepper strawberries. Place the strawberries in a bowl, add the sugar and black pepper and toss together. Leave to macerate for 5–10 minutes.

Scoop the ice cream into shallow dishes and spoon the strawberries beside it. Finish with some rose petals and a little more black pepper, if you fancy.

SUPPER

Espresso Ice Cream Sandwiches
with Ginger Cookies

Makes 8

1 litre (4 cups) coffee ice
    cream (to make your own
    ice cream see page 176)

FOR THE GINGER COOKIES
100 g (3½ oz) butter, plus
    extra for greasing
50 g (2 oz/2 tbsps) black
    treacle
50 g (2 oz/3 tbsps) syrup
    from a jar of stem ginger
100 g (3½ oz/½ cup) light
    brown sugar
150 g (5 oz/1¼ cups) plain
    (all-purpose) flour
50 g (2 oz/⅓ cup)
    wholemeal flour
1 tsp bicarbonate of soda
    (baking soda)
1 tsp ground ginger
½ tsp ground cinnamon
½ tsp ground coriander
½ tsp mixed spice
¼ tsp salt
demerara sugar, for
    dredging

SUBS
light brown sugar – dark
    muscovado
black treacle – date molasses
stem ginger syrup – golden
    syrup
wholemeal flour –
    wholemeal spelt flour

Though espresso ice cream makes an amazing accompaniment to a rich chocolate torte, here I have paired it with these chewy ginger cookies for a slightly lighter pudding. These will keep well in the freezer, so it's good to make a larger batch. Simply allow the biscuits to thaw and soften for 5 minutes before enjoying.

Allow the ice cream to soften for five minutes or so at room temperature, only until it's spoonable, no more.

Grease and line a deep baking tray (pan), about 20 × 30 cm (8 × 12 in). Spoon the softened ice cream into the tray and spread level. Cover with clingfilm (plastic wrap) and place in the freezer for a minimum of 2 hours.

Meanwhile, make the cookies. Preheat the oven to 170°C fan (375°F/gas 5). Line 2 large baking trays with baking paper.

Melt the butter over a medium heat in a small saucepan, then remove from the heat and stir in the treacle and syrup. Whisk to combine.

Place the sugar in a bowl and pour the hot butter mixture on top. Mix to remove any lumps, then add the flours, bicarbonate of soda, spices and salt. Mix to a stiff dough.

Weigh out 30 g (1 oz) pieces of dough (you should get 16–18 pieces), roll into balls, then dredge them in demerara sugar. Arrange on the baking trays, leaving plenty of space for spreading. You may need to bake the biscuits in batches if you don't have space for them all.

Use the flat bottom of a glass to press down on the dough to flatten the cookies a little.

FOR THE ESPRESSO ICE
   CREAM (if not using
   shop-bought)
100 g (3½ oz/scant ½ cup)
   caster (superfine) sugar
75 g (2½ oz/scant ½ cup)
   light brown sugar
8 egg yolks
750 g (1 lb 10 oz/3 cups)
   double (heavy) cream
4 tsps instant espresso
   powder mixed with 100 g
   (3½ oz/scant ½ cup)
   boiling water

Bake for 10–12 minutes, or until just cooked but still slightly soft in the centre. Allow to cool on the trays for 10–15 minutes before transferring to a wire rack to cool completely. The biscuits will keep in an airtight container for up to 5 days.

When ready to serve, remove the ice cream tray from the freezer. Use a round cutter about the size of your cookies to cut out 8 discs of ice cream. (Any ice cream offcuts can be placed in a tub and enjoyed as part of an extra-strong affogato at a later date.) Use 2 cookies to sandwich together the discs of ice cream and serve immediately. If you want to serve later, wrap the sandwiches in greaseproof paper and store in the freezer in an airtight container for up to 1 month. Allow to sit at room temperature for 5–10 minutes before serving.

TO MAKE YOUR OWN ICE CREAM

Whisk together the sugars and the egg yolks in a bowl until combined. Heat the cream in a medium saucepan until just about boiling. Pour the hot cream over the yolk mixture and whisk to combine.

Return the mixture to the pan over a medium-low heat and continuously whisk until the custard reaches 80°C (176°F).

Remove from the heat and whisk in the coffee mixture. I like to use a hand-held blender to emulsify the mixture and make it extra smooth, but this is optional. Set aside to cool down or place the pan in a sink with some ice cubes and cold water to speed up the process.

Once completely chilled, churn in an ice-cream maker according to the manufacturer's instructions. Spoon into the same-sized tray as if using shop-bought ice cream.

Walnut *and* Caramel Tart

Serves 8–10

FOR THE PASTRY

125 g (4 oz) unsalted butter,
  chilled, cubed
200 g (7 oz/1⅔ cups) plain
  (all-purpose) flour
50 g (2 oz/½ cup) ground
  almonds (almond meal)
100 g (3½ oz/generous
  ¾ cup) icing (powdered)
  sugar
1 egg yolk
crème fraîche, to serve

FOR THE FILLING

450 g (1 lb/2 cups) caster
  (superfine) sugar
120 g (4 oz/½ cup) water
300 g (10½ oz/1¼ cups)
  double (heavy) cream
60 g (2¼ oz) unsalted butter
1 tsp vanilla bean paste
240 g (8½ oz/2⅓ cups)
  walnuts
60 g (2¼ oz/⅔ cup) flaked
  (slivered) almonds
¾ tsp salt

SUBS

ground almonds – plain (all-
  purpose) flour
walnuts – pecans;
  hazelnuts; whole almonds
vanilla – 1 tbsp brandy

The sort of tart that will make the sweet toothed very happy indeed.

In the bowl of a food processor, weigh all the pastry ingredients and blitz on a high speed until the mixture resembles a crumble-like consistency. Stop the machine, scrape down the sides and blitz again. Stop when the mixture combines and forms a dough. If this doesn't happen within a quick timeframe, add a tbsp of water and blitz again.

Alternatively, you can do this by hand, working the butter into the flour and icing sugar until you have a sand-like texture. Add the egg yolk, then work gently to bring the dough together. Again, you may need to add a tbsp or so of water to combine.

Once the dough has formed, flatten into a rough rectangle about 2 cm (¾ in) thick. This helps chill the dough faster and makes it easier for you to roll out. Cover with clingfilm (plastic wrap) and rest in the refrigerator for at least 30 minutes. It will keep well in the refrigerator for up to 3 days.

Once chilled, roll out the dough to 2–3 mm (⅛ in) thick. Line a loose-bottomed 23 cm (9 in) tart tin (pan) with the pastry, gently pressing it into the fluted edges. Trim away any excess. Place the lined tin in the freezer for 15 minutes.

Meanwhile, preheat the oven to 190°C fan (410°F/gas 7).

Line the frozen tart with either foil, baking paper or oven-safe clingfilm. Fill with baking beans, or rice, lentils or any other small and cheap dry grain or pulse. Blind bake for 15–20 minutes, or until golden all over. Carefully remove your lining and baking beans.

Meanwhile, prepare your filling. Measure out the sugar and water in a large saucepan. Place over a medium heat and stir until the sugar dissolves. Once dissolved, try your best not to touch it. You can swirl the pan a little to make sure the caramel colours evenly, but avoid stirring it again. Once dark golden and evenly coloured, remove from the heat and gradually add the cream, whisking in between additions to prevent it from spluttering up over the top of the pan. When you have added all of the cream, whisk in the butter and vanilla, then the nuts and the salt.

Pour the filling into the blind-baked tart case. Place in the oven and bake for 20–25 minutes, or until bubbling all over the surface – you are looking for a central temperature of 110–115°C (230°F). Gently remove from the oven and set aside to cool down completely in the tin.

Store in the refrigerator or a cool place for up to 3 days until ready to serve. Allow to come to room temperature for 15 minutes before slicing and plating.

Brown Butter Cakes

Makes 8

100 g (3½ oz) unsalted
    butter, plus extra for
    greasing
100 g (3½ oz/½ cup) light
    brown sugar
2 eggs
100 g (3½ oz/1 cup) ground
    almonds (almond meal)
½ tsp baking powder
20–30 g (¾ oz/2 tbsps)
    (flaked (slivered)
    almonds, for topping

SUBS
light brown sugar – caster
    (superfine) sugar
ground almonds – ground
    hazelnuts

For years I have battled with making financiers, often
to varying degrees of success. I love their buttery-ness,
but often mine turn out claggy and not quite as light as
I would like. I am sure this version doesn't fully classify
as a financier, but I love them as a little sweet bite after
a meal and the brown butter really helps to deliver the
rich buttery flavour I crave.

Preheat the oven to 170°C fan (375°F/gas 5).

Melt the butter in a small saucepan over a medium-high heat
until the butter begins to crackle and splutter – this is the
moisture reacting with the hot fat, so don't worry too much
about it. Stir the butter regularly. At this point you should
notice it begins to foam up. Once the butter stops foaming,
it will start to brown and the milk solids at the bottom of the
pan are dark. Remove from the heat when it reaches a
hazelnut brown colour. Carefully pour the butter through
a metal sieve (strainer) lined with a piece of kitchen paper
into a heatproof mixing bowl. Set aside.

Wipe out the pan to remove the milk solids and return to a
medium heat to melt a small knob of butter. Cut 16 strips of
baking paper, each 15 × 1 cm (6 × ½ in). Use a pastry brush
to liberally brush the holes of an 8-hole muffin tin (pan) with
the melted butter, then press 2 strips of your paper into each
muffin tin in a cross shape, allowing the paper to overhang
the edges. Set aside.

Add the sugar, eggs and ground almonds to the browned
butter and whisk to combine. Add the baking powder and
whisk again until smooth and lump-free. Working quickly,

spoon the mixture into your lined muffin tin, filling each hole three-quarters full. Sprinkle over the flaked almonds.

Bake for 15–18 minutes, or until golden brown and cooked through.

While still warm, run a sharp knife around the side of the cakes to loosen. Allow to cool in the tin for 5–10 minutes, then use the paper strips to gently lift out the cakes.

You can serve these cakes still warm with a nice dollop of extra-thick double (heavy) cream or alongside espressos after a meal. They are equally as tasty at room temperature. Store in an airtight container for up to 2 days.

Sherry *and* Quince Trifle

*Makes 6 individual trifles or
    1 massive trifle*

2 large quince
150 g (5 oz/generous ¾ cup)
    dark muscovado sugar,
    or to taste
400 g (14 oz/generous
    1½ cups) water
1 slice of lemon
1 tsp vanilla bean paste or
    ½ vanilla pod, or to taste
2½ leaves of gelatine
3 tbsps dry sherry
    (I use Leith's Distillery)
250 g (9 oz) Madeira cake,
    cubed (store-bought is
    best for this job, please
    and thank you!)
1–2 400 g (14 oz) tins of
    good-quality custard
300 g (10½ oz/1¼ cups)
    double (heavy) cream

TO DECORATE
toasted flaked (slivered)
    almonds
crushed amaretti biscuits

SUBS
dark muscovado – light
    brown sugar
lemon – orange
Madeira cake – Victoria
    sponge; almond loaf;
    lemon loaf

If you aren't using store-bought custard or cake for a trifle, then I would argue you are not a nostalgic person. Some things genuinely taste better when not homemade and trifle is one of those rare examples that truly benefits from a store-bought sponge.

Peel, core and slice the quince into wedges. Place in a shallow pan with the sugar, water, lemon and vanilla. Cover with a lid or a piece of greaseproof paper and simmer for 30–45 minutes over a low heat, or until the quince are soft and tender but still holding their shape. Spoon out the fruit and set aside.

Taste the remaining syrup, adding more vanilla or sugar if necessary. Measure out 225 g (8 oz/scant 1 cup) of the syrup (top up with a little water or sherry if you are short).

Soak the gelatine leaves in cold water.

Return the measured syrup to a simmer, then remove from the heat. Add the soaked gelatine and stir to combine.

In your serving glasses or bowl, add the cake cubes and the cooled quince slices. You can slice the quince as finely or thickly as you like here. Spoon over the sherry, dividing it equally. Top up with the quince syrup. Place in the refrigerator to set for 1 hour.

Once set, spoon over your custard. Softly whip the cream (you can add more vanilla or booze with the cream) and gently spoon on top. Finish with toasted flaked almonds and some crushed amaretti biscuits. Eat immediately.

You can make the jelly and quince ahead of time, then simply assemble the custard and cream on top just before serving.

Tiramisu

Makes 4–6 individual
   tiramisu

2 eggs

50 g (2 oz/¼ cup) light
   brown sugar

250 g (9 oz) mascarpone

2 tbsps espresso powder
   mixed with 100 g (3½ oz/
   scant ½ cup) boiling
   water

100 g (3½ oz/scant ½ cup)
   marsala or a good-quality
   coffee liqueur of your
   choosing

8–12 lady fingers (sponge
   fingers) (about 100 g/
   3½ oz)

cocoa powder, for dusting

SUBS

light brown sugar – caster
   (superfine) sugar

booze – espresso

cocoa – grated chocolate

A chef friend once told me that booze isn't traditional in tiramisu. The history of tiramisu in Italy seems so fraught with various regions wanting to claim it that to bring a contentious subject of alcohol into it might be a step too far. Regardless of whether or not it is traditional, I firmly believe it can be included. If you don't drink, replace the alcohol with the same volume of extra espresso.

Place the eggs and sugar in a freestanding mixer fitted with the whisk attachment and whisk on a high speed for 5–8 minutes, or until thick, pale and more than tripled in volume. You can also do this with an electric hand mixer.

In a separate bowl, beat the mascarpone to loosen it a little. Mix together the espresso and the booze, then pour 3 tbsps of the mixture in with the mascarpone. Mix again to combine.

Break the lady fingers in half and place 4 halves in the bottom of each ramekin or glass. (I like to use old-fashioned champagne glasses for this or a variety of different etched glasses, but it is entirely up to you, and how many puddings you make will vary depending on your glass size. For mini ones, you may only need 2 lady finger halves.) Spoon over the remaining coffee mixture, dividing equally between the glasses, and allow the sponges to soak up the coffee.

Once the eggs have become pale and fluffy, gently fold into the mascarpone mixture in 3 batches, being careful not to knock out too much air. Divide between your glasses. Dust the tops generously with cocoa powder and place in the refrigerator for at least 2 hours or ideally overnight.

These will keep well in the refrigerator for up to 3–4 days (I actually think they taste better after this time).

Brown Sugar Cheesecake

Makes a 20 cm (8 in)
  cheesecake

FOR THE BASE
350 g (12 oz) gingernut
  biscuits
100 g (3½ oz) butter,
  softened, plus extra for
  greasing

FOR THE FILLING
200 g (7 oz) butter
250 g (9 oz/1⅓ cups) light
  brown sugar
340 g (11½ oz) full-fat cream
  cheese
500 g (1 lb 2 oz) mascarpone
50 g (2 oz/3 tbsps) double
  (heavy) cream
4 eggs
1 tsp vanilla bean paste
1 tbsp date molasses
  (optional)

SUBS
gingernut biscuits –
  digestives (Graham
  crackers)
mascarpone – more cream
  cheese

I much prefer a baked cheesecake. I often find the set ones are cloying and don't have the smooth creaminess you get with a baked version. That being said, they do tend to be quite a bit more hassle, especially when it comes to the bake times. Don't be tempted to rush this stage and make sure you set timers to reduce the temperature each time.

Preheat the oven to 170°C fan (375°F/gas 5). Grease and line a loose-bottomed 20 cm (8 in) cake tin (pan).

Place the gingernut biscuits and softened butter into a food processor and blitz until fine. There's no need to melt the butter.

Tip the mixture out of the bowl and press into the lined tin. Bake for 10–15 minutes (this step is optional but recommended if you want a nice crisp base).

Meanwhile, weigh out the butter and light brown sugar into the same food processor (no need to clean it in between these steps). Blitz on a high speed until well combined and pale in colour. Add the cream cheese, mascarpone and double cream, and blitz again, making sure you scrape down the sides in between so that everything is incorporated. Add the eggs, vanilla and date molasses, if using, and blitz again until smooth and combined. If your mixture splits at any point, simply continue to blitz until it re-emulsifies.

Pour the cheesecake mixture over the baked base and place in the oven. Turn the oven down immediately to 150°C fan (340°F/gas 3) and bake for 30 minutes.

After this time, turn the oven down to 120°C fan (275°F/gas ½) and bake for a further 30 minutes.

Finally, turn the oven down to 100°C fan (240°F/gas ¼) and bake for a final 30 minutes or until the cheesecake is just set, with a small wobble in the middle. Allow to cool completely before placing in the refrigerator for up to 3 days.

When ready to serve, use a sharp knife dipped in boiling water to get clean slices.

Buttermilk Panna Cotta
with Boozy Greengages

Makes 4-6 panna cottas

FOR THE PANNA COTTAS
1½ sheets of gelatine (2 if
   you want a firmer set)

225 g (8 oz/scant 1 cup)
   double (heavy) cream
90 g (3¼ oz/generous ⅓ cup)
   caster (superfine) sugar
1 tsp vanilla bean paste or
   ½ vanilla pod
225 g (8 oz/scant 1 cup)
   buttermilk (see method
   on page 192 to make your
   own)

FOR THE BOOZY
   GREENGAGES
8-10 greengages (about
   200 g /7 oz)
45 g (1¾ oz/¼ cup) light
   brown sugar
3 tbsps brandy
1 tbsp water *(optional)*
whole roasted almonds,
   roughly chopped (30-40 g/
   1-1½ oz), to decorate

SUBS
greengages – plums; figs
light brown sugar – caster
   (superfine) sugar
brandy – sherry

The greengages can easily be swapped here for another stone fruit. If you have the time, I would also encourage you to make your own buttermilk. It's simple to do and wonderfully rewarding!

Soak the gelatine in a bowl of cold water for 5-10 minutes.

For the panna cottas, heat 125 g (4 oz) of the cream, sugar and vanilla together in a medium saucepan until just beginning to boil. Remove from the heat. Squeeze the gelatine sheets to remove any excess water, then add to the hot cream mixture and allow to sit for 10 minutes to cool down a little. Stir in the remaining cream and the buttermilk and whisk until smooth.

Pour into ramekins or pudding moulds (use nonreactive metal moulds) and leave to cool for 15 minutes. Place in the refrigerator and refrigerate for at least 4 hours, but ideally overnight. They can be kept refrigerated for up to 3 days.

For the boozy greengages, slice the fruit in half and remove the pits. Heat a small frying pan (skillet) over a medium heat and place the fruit in cut-sides down. Sprinkle over the sugar and cook for a minute or so until the fruit begins to colour. Add the brandy and turn the heat down. Shake the pan to coat the fruit and melt the sugar. You can flambé the fruit if you like at this point. Add a splash of water if your sauce has thickened and remove from the heat. You don't want to overcook the fruit, as they may lose their shape, so err on the side of caution. Taste the syrup and adjust accordingly (you can add a little vanilla or a squeeze of orange juice to it, if you like).

To serve, dip the panna cottas into a bowl of boiling water and allow to sit for a few seconds (if you have made them in ramekins you may need to leave them for longer or use a knife to begin to loosen them). Place a serving plate over the top of each panna cotta, then flip over quickly.

You may need to give them a jiggle to get them out of the moulds. Spoon over a few of the greengages and a little of the syrup and decorate with the almonds.

The greengages will keep for up to 3 days in the refrigerator.

TO MAKE YOUR OWN BUTTERMILK

560 g (20 oz/2½ cups) (600 ml pot) double (heavy) cream

Place the cream in a freestanding mixer fitted with the whisk attachment. Whip the cream on a high speed until thickened. Once whipped, lower the speed and continue to whisk – it will begin to look a little lumpy. Cover with a dish towel and keep mixing until the mixture has completely split (the towel will help stop you from getting splashed with buttermilk!).

Strain the mixture into a bowl. The liquid is buttermilk; the butter fat will remain in the sieve. Squeeze the solids with your hands to get rid of any excess buttermilk, then wash the butter under cold water. Keep squeezing to get rid of any excess liquid. Pat dry. You can season with a little salt at this point or simply wrap with greaseproof paper and store in the refrigerator to bake or cook with as unsalted butter.

TO MAKE PANNA COTTA WITH CARAMEL

Melt 150 g (5 oz/⅔ cup) caster (superfine) sugar in a large saucepan over a medium heat. Do not be tempted to stir, simply swirl the pan to make sure it all melts evenly. Continue to cook until it turns a golden amber colour. Pour into the base of your pudding moulds or ramekins and allow to set before pouring over your panna cotta mix. Cool in the refrigerator overnight before turning out.

Baked Apples
and Pine Nut Crumble

Serves 2

2 small eating apples

1 strip of lemon zest

½ vanilla pod

¼ tsp fennel seeds

4 large fennel flowers
   (optional)

1 rosemary sprig

50 g (2 oz/2 tbsps) honey

25 g (¾ oz) butter

small pinch of salt

yoghurt or crème fraîche,
   or double (heavy) cream,
   to serve

FOR THE CRUMBLE

50 g (2 oz) butter

50 g (2 oz/¼ cup) light
   brown sugar

50 g (2 oz/⅓ cup)
   wholemeal flour

25 g (¾ oz/¼ cup) ground
   almonds (almond meal)

50 g (2 oz) pine nuts

SUBS

lemon – orange

rosemary – bay leaves

wholemeal flour – spelt flour;
   plain (all-purpose) flour

Cooking apples in a parcel is a brilliant way to use their natural sweetness to create a syrupy sauce. Serve on the table in their parcel and people can help themselves.

Preheat the oven to 180°C fan (400°F/gas 6). Place a large sheet of greaseproof paper over 2 sheets of foil.

Slice the apples in half horizontally and place in the middle of the greaseproof paper. Add the lemon zest, vanilla pod, fennel and rosemary. Drizzle over the honey and add the butter. Sprinkle with a tiny amount of salt. Fold the foil over the fruit to meet the opposite side and fold over the edges. Fold again to create a tight seal. Double fold the sides in the same way to form a tightly sealed parcel.

Bake for 45 minutes, or until the apples feel soft and are just holding their shape.

Meanwhile, make the crumble. Blitz together the butter, sugar, flour and almonds in a food processor until it has a sandy consistency. Tip into a bowl and add the pine nuts. Scrunch together to create lumps much like you get with granola. Tip onto a baking sheet and place in the oven with the apples. Bake for 5–10 minutes before removing and mixing. Return to the oven and mix again in 5 minutes. Repeat this process until the crumble is golden brown and crisp.

To serve, spoon a good dollop of yoghurt or crème fraîche into each bowl. Spoon 2 apple halves onto the yoghurt along with any cooking juices, then spoon a generous amount of crumble on top. Finish with a drizzle of double cream à la my grandfather (the king of double dairy).

CHAPTER SEVEN

Let's do it all *again*

Monday-Night Soup

Serves 4

olive oil, for cooking
1 banana shallot, finely
  sliced
2 spring onions (scallions),
  finely sliced
2 garlic cloves, finely sliced
1 kg (2 lb 4 oz/4 cups)
  chicken stock
50 g (2 oz) chard or another
  leafy green, finely sliced
10 g (1/2 oz) flat-leaf parsley,
  finely sliced
5 g (1/4 oz) tarragon, finely
  sliced
200 g (7 oz) chicken meat
  picked from a leftover
  roast chicken carcass
stelline pasta or pearl
  couscous *(optional)*

SUBS
spring onions – ⅓ leek
parsley – chervil

Simple and soothing for the tiredness that all too often accompanies a Monday evening.

Heat a little oil in a saucepan and sweat the shallot, spring onions and garlic over a medium heat until softened.

Strain the chicken stock through a muslin-lined colander, then add it to the pan along with the chard, parsley, tarragon and chicken meat. Simmer for 5 minutes before serving.

You can add some stelline pasta or pearl couscous in for the last few minutes of cooking to bulk this recipe up, but you may require extra stock. If you have used the leftovers from the Spatchcock Chicken recipe on page 116, spoon a little excess parsley mayo on top of the broth just before serving.

Crispy Lamb
and Chickpea Pancakes

Serves 2

FOR THE PANCAKES

125 g (4 oz/scant 1 cup)
  chickpea flour (besan), or
  as needed
1 tbsp cornflour (cornstarch)
½ tsp ground cumin
250 g (9 oz/1 cup) water
3 tbsps milk
small handful of coriander
  (cilantro) leaves
pinch of salt
olive oil, for cooking

FOR THE SALAD

1 carrot, peeled into ribbons
5 g (¼ oz) coriander
  (cilantro), finely chopped
1 tsp black sesame seeds
1 tsp white sesame seeds
1 tbsp lime juice
3 tbsps peanut oil

FOR THE CRISPY TOPPING

olive oil, for cooking
4 spring onions (scallions),
  finely sliced
½ small green chilli, finely
  sliced
2 garlic cloves, finely sliced
1 tsp ground coriander
150 g (5 oz) leftover lamb,
  shredded (chicken works
  here too)
30 g (1 oz/3 tbsps) salted
  and roasted cashew
  nuts, chopped

You can really top these pancakes with anything you like. I love their savoury lightness and soft, supple texture – almost like a French buckwheat crêpe. These are brilliant for enjoying early on in the week to use up the last of the weekend's roast.

To make the pancake batter, place all of the ingredients (except the oil) in a food processor and blitz. It should resemble crêpe batter. Set aside.

For the salad, combine all the ingredients in a bowl and toss to combine.

For the crispy topping, heat a little oil in a frying pan (skillet), over a medium heat and add the spring onions, chilli and the garlic, and cook for 5 minutes or until softened. Add the coriander and the lamb with a splash of water, increase the heat and cook until everything is beginning to crisp up. Add the chopped cashews and heat for a minute or two, then remove the pan from the heat. Set your topping aside and keep warm.

To make the pancakes (mixture will make 2–4), clean the frying pan then heat a little olive oil in the pan over a medium heat. Spoon in a ladleful of the batter and swirl the pan so it coats the base. Be careful not to overfill the pan as the pancake is more likely to crack – you want a thin pancake. Cook for roughly 1 minute, then flip when nearly cooked through. Cook for a further 30 seconds or until just cooked through, then place in a clean dish towel to keep warm. Repeat with the rest of the batter, making sure you add a little more oil in between each one. It is important to cook the pancakes last as they often dry out and crack if left too long.

TO SERVE
coriander (cilantro) leaves
lime wedges
yoghurt

SUBS
spring onions – banana
    shallot
cashew nuts – roasted
    almonds; salted and
    roasted peanuts
peanut oil – sesame oil

To assemble, place a warm pancake on each plate, then top
with some salad. Spoon the hot crispy lamb over one half
of the pancake. Garnish with some coriander leaves, a few
wedges of lime and a little dollop of yoghurt, then fold the
top over lightly. Eat immediately.

Potato *and* Saffron Stew

Serves 2–4

olive oil, for cooking

2 shallots, finely sliced

1 leek, finely sliced

1 fennel bulb, finely sliced

4 garlic cloves, finely sliced

400 g (14 oz) cooked
  potatoes, halved if small
  or quartered if large

¼ tsp smoked paprika

500 g (1 lb 2 oz/2 cups)
  chicken stock (page 208)

3–5 saffron threads

2 thyme sprigs

2 rosemary sprigs

1 roasted red pepper from a
  jar, sliced into 2.5 cm
  (1 in) strips

50 g (2 oz/scant ½ cup)
  black olives, coarsely
  chopped

salt and freshly ground
  black pepper

TO SERVE
bread
aioli

SUBS
leek – more shallots
chicken stock – veg stock
black olives – green olives;
  20 g (¾ oz) capers

I often overdo it on the potato front, so this is a helpful recipe to reach for when too much mashed or fried potatoes, or bubble and squeak, have been made. It will work equally as well with leftover roasted potatoes, too.

Heat a little oil in a large saucepan over a medium heat. Add the shallots, leek and fennel and cook for 10–15 minutes, then add the garlic, potatoes and paprika. Cook for a few minutes, then pour in the stock.

Bloom the saffron in a small dish with a splash of very hot water, letting it sit for a few minutes. Add to the pan with the thyme and rosemary. Season and leave to simmer for 20 minutes.

Stir the pepper and olives into the stew, taste and adjust the seasoning.

Serve with some good bread and a dollop of aioli on top.

SUPPER

Chicken, Baby Gem
and Gravy Dressing

Serves 4

3 small baby gem lettuce

a drizzle of olive oil

20 g (¾ oz/3 tbsps) walnuts,
  roughly chopped

20 g (¾ oz/3 tbsps) pumpkin
  seeds, roughly chopped

300 g (10½ oz) chicken
  meat, picked from a
  leftover roast

5 g (¼ oz) chervil, leaves
  picked

1 tarragon sprig, leaves
  picked

4 anchovy fillets

zest of ½ lemon

20 g (¾ oz) Parmesan,
  finely grated

50 g (2 oz/¼ cup) crème
  fraîche

freshly ground black pepper

FOR THE GRAVY DRESSING

3 tbsps leftover gravy

juice of ½ lemon

3 tbsps olive oil

SUBS

Parmesan – Grana Padano;
  pecorino

anchovies – capers

chervil – parsley

walnuts – almonds

My take on a Caesar salad, minus the heaviness that a
thick, creamy dressing normally brings. Croutons can also
be added if you want the more classic style. Alternatively,
sprinkle over some Pangrattato (see page 212).

Heat a griddle pan over a high heat. Quarter two of the baby
gem lettuce and drizzle with a little olive oil. Place cut-sides
down on the griddle and leave until charred, then turn to char
the other cut sides. Set aside.

To make the dressing, whisk together the gravy, lemon juice
and oil. Check for seasoning, adding a little more lemon if
it needs more acidity, or oil if it's too strong (this will all depend
on your gravy).

In a small frying pan (skillet), toast the nuts and the seeds
until golden and fragrant.

To serve, break up the leaves of the final lettuce and arrange
on a large serving platter, then arrange the charred lettuce
in among the leaves. Scatter over the picked chicken and
herbs. Break up the anchovies a little and sprinkle over the
dish, then sprinkle over the lemon zest and half of the toasted
nuts and seeds. Drizzle over the dressing, then finish with
the grated Parmesan, the remaining nuts and seeds, and some
dollops of crème fraîche. Finish with a crack of black pepper.

NOTE

If you have any chicken skin left over, try crisping it up in
a frying pan. Simply stretch out onto the pan, cover with a
sheet of baking paper and place a saucepan slightly smaller
than the frying pan on top to weigh it down. Cook over a
medium heat until golden and crisp throughout.

Arancini

Makes 12–16 balls

250 g (9 oz) leftover risotto,
   chilled (see Barley
   Risotto recipe on
   page 66)
250 g (9 oz) buffalo
   mozzarella
50 g (2 oz) Parmesan, finely
   grated, plus extra to serve
2 eggs
plain (all-purpose) flour,
   for dredging
panko breadcrumbs,
   for coating
sunflower oil, for deep-frying
salt and freshly ground
   black pepper
marjoram and chive flowers,
   to serve

SUBS
Parmesan – Cheddar
panko – stale bread blitzed
   into breadcrumbs

All too often, these are the reason I make risotto in the first place. I have never met a crusted and cheesy deep-fried item I didn't like.

Mix together the risotto with the mozzarella and Parmesan. This can be quite roughly done, as you don't want to overmix it. Season if required. Store in the refrigerator until ready to roll.

When ready to roll, whisk the eggs in a bowl, add some seasoned flour to another bowl, and lastly add some panko breadcrumbs to a third bowl.

Roll the risotto mixture into 12–16 × 30 g (1 oz) balls. First, roll them in a little flour, then dust off the excess. Coat each one in some egg, then return to the flour and coat again. Coat once more in egg, then cover in panko breadcrumbs. It's important to 'double dunk' the balls, so they get a good coating on them to prevent the mozzarella from leaking out when frying. Repeat with the rest of the balls.

Fill a deep saucepan with a 5–7 cm (2–3 in) depth of sunflower oil and heat until it reaches 170°C (338°F). Add the arancini, being careful not to overcrowd the pan, and cook for 4–5 minutes, or until golden brown and piping hot throughout. Remove with a slotted spoon to drain on a piece of kitchen paper and season with a little salt. Repeat until they are all cooked.

Serve immediately with some finely grated Parmesan over the top and some marjoram or chive flowers.

Stocks *and* Broths

Makes roughly 2 litres,
but this will depend on
how much you reduce
your stock by

2–3 banana shallots

1 carrot

1 leek

1 celery stalk

1 cooked chicken carcass,
meat picked off

3 thyme sprigs

3 rosemary sprigs

2 bay leaves

6 black peppercorns

6 garlic cloves

One of the main joys of dining at home is the possibilities for leftovers, be that simply enjoying last night's dinner for lunch the following day or using them to create a whole other dining experience. Making stocks is the best way to get the ball rolling again and begin planning a new feast.

Chop the veg into quarters and place in a large saucepan with the chicken carcass. Add the remaining ingredients, then cover with water until everything is submerged. Bring to a simmer and cook for 2–3 hours, ensuring it doesn't boil. The stock is ready when it is flavoursome and reduced by roughly a third.

Strain and use with 2 days, or freeze for use later on.

BEEF – replace the chicken with 1–1.5 kg (2 lb 4 oz–3 lb 5 oz) beef bones (ask your butcher).

LAMB – replace the chicken with 1–1.2 kg (2 lb 4 oz–2 lb 14 oz) lamb bones, replace the leek with ¼ celeriac (celery root) and add 6 juniper berries.

FISH – replace the chicken with 1 kg (2 lb 4 oz) white fish bones (oily fish such as tuna and mackerel won't make for a good stock), replace the carrot with another celery stalk, replace the leek with ½ fennel bulb, replace the thyme with dill and the rosemary with tarragon, add 100 g (3½ oz/scant ½ cup) white wine and ½ lemon cut into slices.

FOR THE LOVE
OF A LEFTOVER PIE

PORK AND CELERIAC PIE

Serves 4

olive oil and butter, for cooking

3 banana shallots, finely sliced

100 g (3½ oz) smoked bacon lardons

10 sage leaves, finely sliced

400 g (14 oz) cooked pork, cut into rough chunks

200 g (7 oz/scant 1 cup) cider

200 g (7 oz/scant 1 cup) chicken stock
(page 208), or as needed

1 tsp grainy mustard

50 g (2 oz) brown bread, blitzed into fine crumbs

50 g (2 oz) double cream

75 g (2½ oz) butter

200–300 g (7–10½ oz) celeriac (celery root),
coarsely grated (it will depend on the size of
your pie dish)

salt and freshly ground black pepper

SUBS

bacon lardons – streaky bacon cut into small
slices

cider – 100 g (3½ oz/scant ½ cup) calvados,
plus top up the stock to 300 g (10½ oz/1¼ cups)

celeriac – parsnip; potatoes

Preheat the oven to 180°C fan (350°F/ gas 4).

Heat a large saucepan with 1–2 tbsp olive oil and a generous knob of butter over a medium heat. Add the shallots and cook for 10 minutes, or until golden brown and softened. Remove from the pan and set aside.

Add the bacon lardons to the pan and cook to render the fat. Add the sage leaves, return the shallots to the pan and add the pork. Pour in the cider and cook for a minute or two before adding the stock and the mustard. Season, then cover with a lid and simmer for 20 minutes until the sauce is thickened a little. Add a little more stock if it reduces too much.

Add the breadcrumbs and cream, stir to combine, then transfer to a pie dish.

Melt the butter in a pan and stir through the grated celeriac. Season, then spoon over the top of the pie to cover.

Bake for 30–40 minutes, or until golden brown and the celeriac has cooked through.

CHICKEN AND FENNEL PIE

Serves 4

FOR THE PASTRY

275 g (10 oz/2¼ cups) plain
   (all-purpose) flour, plus extra for dusting
2 tsps baking powder
½ tsp salt
¼ tsp freshly ground black pepper
100 g (3½ oz) suet
200 g (7 oz/scant 1 cup)
   ice-cold water

FOR THE FILLING

olive oil, for cooking
2 white onions, finely sliced
1 fennel bulb, finely sliced
2 tbsps wholemeal flour
330ml (11 oz) can of pale ale
200 g (7 oz/scant 1 cup) chicken stock
400 g (14 oz) cooked chicken
2 thyme sprigs
2 marjoram sprigs
5 g (¼ oz) fennel fronds, finely chopped
5 g (¼ oz) flat-leaf parsley, finely chopped
salt and freshly ground black pepper

TO FINISH

1 egg
fennel seeds

SUBS

suet – butter; lard
pale ale – 100 g (3½ oz/scant ½ cup) dry sherry

For the pastry, mix together the flour, baking powder, salt and pepper in a bowl. Add the suet and rub it into the flour. Pour in the water a little at a time and use a butter knife to mix the dough and begin to bind it. Once starting to form a dough, knead together very gently until the flour has just been absorbed. Flatten into a disc, cover with clingfilm (plastic wrap) and refrigerate for 1 hour.

Preheat the oven to 180°C (350°F/gas 4).

For the filling, heat a little oil in a large saucepan over a medium heat. Add the onions and fennel and cook for 10 minutes until softened and golden. Add the flour and stir to coat. Pour in the ale and cook for a few minutes, then add the stock, chicken, thyme and marjoram, and season. Cover with a lid and simmer for 20 minutes or so.

On a lightly dusted work surface, roll out your pastry to 3–4 mm (⅛ in) thick. Beat the egg lightly.

Once the filling has thickened, add the chopped herbs and season to taste. Pour into your pie dish. Brush the edges of the dish with a little egg, then cover with the pastry. Trim off any excess. Crimp the edges using your thumb and index fingers, then brush all over with the egg. Cut a small cross in the middle to release any steam. Sprinkle over a small amount of fennel seeds. Bake for 30 minutes, or until the pastry is crisp, shiny and golden brown.

LENTIL AND POTATO PIE

Serves 4–6

olive oil, for cooking and drizzling
½ leek, finely sliced
1 carrot, finely diced
2 banana shallots, finely sliced
3 garlic cloves, finely sliced
1 tsp ground cumin
1 tsp ground coriander
½ tsp ground cinnamon
½ tsp ground turmeric
2 tsps nigella seeds
½ tsp yellow mustard seeds
1 x 400 g (14 oz) tin plum tomatoes
1 vegetable stock cube
100 g (3½ oz/½ cup) green lentils
salt and freshly ground black pepper

FOR THE TOPPING
500 g (1 lb 2 oz) leftover cooked potatoes
75 g (2½ oz) butter
75 g (2½ oz/5 tbsps) milk
salt and freshly ground black pepper
nigella seeds, to finish

SUBS
leek – 4 spring onions (scallions)
green lentils – Puy lentils
milk – cream; oat milk

Preheat the oven to 200°C (400°F/gas 6).

Heat a little olive oil in a large saucepan over a medium heat and add the leek, carrot and shallots. Cook for 10–15 minutes or until softened and golden. Add the garlic and cook for a few more minutes before adding all of the spices. Stir through and cook for 2 minutes. Add the tomatoes, then refill the tin with water and add to the pan and crumble in the stock cube. Add the lentils and season. Cover the pan with a lid and simmer for 30 minutes, stirring occasionally.

Meanwhile, mash the potatoes for the topping with a fork. Melt the butter with the milk and pour into the potatoes, season and mix well until fluffy (the mixture doesn't need to be completely smooth).

When the lentils are just about cooked, spoon into a pie dish. Spoon dollops of your potatoes on top (it doesn't need to be perfect; I quite like little blips of sauce coming up through the top of the potatoes). Drizzle with oil, then sprinkle over some nigella seeds.

Bake in the oven for 30 minutes, or until golden and crunchy on top.

Pangrattato

150 g (5 oz) stale bread (any
    type is fine, although I
    find a seeded loaf works
    very well here)
½ tsp chilli (hot pepper)
    flakes
4 anchovy fillets
zest of ½ lemon
2 garlic cloves, minced
4–6 large sage leaves
½ tsp salt
½ tsp freshly ground
    black pepper
olive oil, for cooking, as
    needed

SUBS
chilli flakes – 1 small fresh
    chilli, deseeded and finely
    chopped
anchovies – 2 tsps capers
sage – rosemary

This is best used to garnish pasta dishes, but I have also served it with potatoes, roast chicken, strews and braised beans before. Anything that requires a bit of a kick and some texture will get on famously with this recipe! I like to collect old heels of bread for this and keep them in the freezer until I have enough to make a double batch of this. Simply defrost and blitz as instructed.

Place the bread in a food processor and blitz until you get small breadcrumbs (they don't need to be perfect). Add the rest of the ingredients, except the olive oil, and blitz again until well combined.

Heat a generous amount of olive oil in a large heavy-based frying pan (skillet) over a medium heat. Once hot, tip in the breadcrumbs and begin to fry. Try to avoid doing this over too high a heat, as the breadcrumbs can catch quickly and unevenly. Continue to cook, adding more olive oil if required, until golden and crisp. Tip onto a plate lined with some kitchen paper to soak up any excess oil and allow to cool down.

Store in an airtight container for up to 2 weeks.

Gremolata

Serves 2-4

½ lemon

30 g (1 oz) mixed soft herbs,
    stalks and all

2 garlic cloves

pinch of salt

The perfect use for old herbs, this adds a freshness when sprinkled on top of salads, roasts or even soups. Although parsley is traditional here, most leafy green herbs will work too. If you don't use it all up on the day it was made, spoon into an ice-cube tray and top up with oil. Freeze, then use when cooking – I like to stir it into pots of beans or hearty stews.

Peel the lemon using a vegetable peeler. Finely chop the lemon peel, herbs and garlic together. This takes a while, but it is the best way to release the flavour. Simply use a large knife and work your way back and forth over the chopping board until the mixture is fine enough. Season with a little pinch of salt.

Store in the refrigerator until ready to use as a garnish.

Old Cake Ice Cream

Makes roughly 1 litre

280 g (10 oz/generous 1 cup)
   double (heavy) cream
120 g (4 oz/½ cup) whole
   (full-fat) milk
2 tsps vanilla bean paste
   or ½ vanilla pod
50 g (2 oz/¼ cup) caster
   (superfine) sugar
3 egg yolks
1 tbsp brandy
150 g (5 oz) stale cake
50 g (2 oz/¼ cup) light
   brown sugar

SUBS
brandy – rum
light brown sugar – caster
   (superfine) sugar

It's very rare that there is cake left in our house. However, I am reliably told that some people struggle to get through a whole sponge between two in a few days, and leftover cake does break my heart. Here is a solution!

Heat the cream and milk with the vanilla in a medium saucepan until just about to boil.

Whisk together the caster sugar and egg yolks in a bowl. Pour the hot cream mixture over the eggs and whisk to combine.

Pour back into the saucepan over a low heat. Whisk constantly until it reaches 82°C (180°F). Set aside to cool down, ideally quickly, so over an ice bath is ideal. Once cool, whisk in the brandy. Store in an airtight container in the refrigerator for at least 1 hour or up to 24 hours.

Preheat the oven to 180°C (350°F/gas 4). Line a baking tray (pan) with baking paper.

Cut the cake into smallish cubes. Mix together with the brown sugar and place on the baking tray. Bake for 10 minutes, or until begin to crisp up and the sugar starts to caramelise. Allow to cool down.

Churn your custard in an ice-cream maker according to the manufacturer's instructions. A few minutes before the ice cream is ready, add the baked cake crumbs and allow to mix and incorporate. Do not overmix at this stage. Once ready, spoon into an airtight container and store in the freezer.

This will work with most sponges and you can add to the ice cream as well: swirled chocolate sauce (page 164) or fruit compote; roasted or roughly chopped hazelnuts.

Shortbread Crumble

Serves 4

200 g (7 oz) leftover
shortbread biscuits
125 g (4 oz) butter
25 g (¾ oz/2 tbsps)
demerara sugar
25 g (¾ oz/¼ cup) ground
almonds (almond meal)
25 g (¾ oz/¼ cup) oats
400 g (14 oz) plums
100 g (3½ oz) brambles
100 g (3½ oz/½ cup)
light brown sugar (adjust
depending on how tart or
sweet your fruit is)
1 ball of stem ginger

SUBS

ground almonds – plain (all-
purpose) or spelt flour
plums – apples
brambles – raspberries

Shortbread and oats in a crumble might sound like an
excessively Scottish variation, but it is a brilliant one,
I promise!

Preheat the oven to 170°C (340°F/gas 3).

Bash the shortbread biscuits into chunky crumbs.

Melt the butter and add to the shortbread along with the
sugar, almonds and oats. Mix everything together – I find
doing this with my hands is best. Set aside.

Halve the plums (or quarter if they are on the big side) and
place in a bowl with the brambles and sugar. Finely chop the
stem ginger and add to the bowl, then muddle together. Spoon
into a cast-iron frying pan (skillet) or any other ovenproof dish,
such as a pie tin or deep roasting tray. Sprinkle over the
crumble topping.

Bake for 20–30 minutes, or until golden brown with deep
purple syrup blipping up around the edges.

Serve with the silky custard on page 167.

Panettone *and* Pistachio Pudding

Serves 4–6

350 g (12 oz) panettone
280 g (10 oz/generous 1 cup)
  double (heavy) cream
2 eggs, plus 2 egg yolks
100 g (3½ oz/½ cup) caster
  (superfine) sugar
25 g (¾ oz) pistachio paste
1 tsp vanilla bean paste
30 g (1 oz/¼ cup) pistachios
  demerara sugar, for
  sprinkling

SUBS
panettone – brioche;
  pandoro
pistachio paste – very finely
  ground pistachios
  (although the flavour
  won't be as intense and
  they will add texture to
  the custard)

Pistachio paste is a pretty luxurious item, but I highly recommend it if you can get your hands on some (it's available online). I like to make this pudding in the days after Christmas, when the panettone has started to go a little stale, but it would be equally good year-round with brioche.

Preheat the oven to 160°C (320°F/gas 2).

Cut the panettone into rough chunks and arrange in a deep roasting dish (you want them to be quite snug and compact).

Heat the cream until just about to boil.

Whisk the eggs, yolks, caster sugar and pistachio paste together with the vanilla until smooth and well combined. Pour the hot cream on top, whisking well. Pour the mixture over the panettone. Chop the pistachios and sprinkle over the top along with some demerara sugar.

Bake for 30 minutes, or until golden and just set in the middle. You can cover with foil if the centre is still too soft but the top is beginning to colour too much.

Index

Acknowledgements

Thank you first and foremost for buying this book and reading about my love affair with all things Supper. We have all changed our way of eating, dining and gathering together so much during the past few years. I truly hope this book encourages you back to the table once more.

The thing I love most about writing cookbooks is the winding road you take, adding and altering what you initially set out to create, as you go. This process is only doable thanks to all the brilliant people that join you and help turn whatever small idea you had into something tangible. I have once again been extremely lucky to be surrounded by phenomenal amounts of talent, and women so skilled I am always left in awe of them.

Laura, I recently found some old screenshots of your work on my phone from 2014. I remember thinking they were the most beautiful pictures I had ever seen. Over eight years and three books later, your work is still the most glorious vision. How infuriating that you are also a wonderfully loving, caring and thoughtful person too. Thank you, thank you, thank you.

Jo, it was so wonderful to meet you properly and run wild around Yorkshire together. Laura has always spoken so highly of you and it's no wonder why. Your help, enthusiasm, encouragement and assistance is massively appreciated and I am very grateful for your input.

Tab, I feel so lucky to have been allowed to muddle through this process for a third time so that I could work with you again. Being greeted by you makes all the hard graft and late nights worthwhile. As usual you understood what I was aiming for impeccably and your aesthetic, napkin laying, eagerness and sun bathing props will always be my favourite.

Rosie, as always your skill, effortlessness and eye left me feeling both fortunate and inspired in equal measure. I adore learning from you and I am so grateful you not only joined our team once more, but also that you hosted us, fed us, cared for us and let us soak up the most glorious time in your home. A week of total joy thanks to your generosity.

El, what a treat to have you on the team! Thank you so much for cooking so beautifully and for your help on all three shoots. We truly couldn't have done Scotland without you. It was a complete honour to have your invaluable input.

Kajal, oh we missed you so! Thank you so much for developing the very beginnings of an idea with me over many months and for always being the lady I want to work with. And now we have an extra pair of hands in the form of little O to help with the next one. Thank you for always understanding me.

Clare and Alicia, thank you both for all your hard work and making sense of my many emails and ideas. It is hugely appreciated.

Chelsea and the whole team at Hardie Grant, thank you for taking the reins and steering me in the right direction. I know it takes a huge amount of work and people squirrelling away in the background and it has not gone unnoticed.

Team ARAN, Team LÒN and Team Shedden, thank you, thank you, thank you. For always putting up with me – even when I disappear upstairs to sit and write for hours on end, or to the other end of the country for photos. The show wouldn't run without you all, especially during the juggle that has been these past few years. I am eternally grateful for your support, tolerance and graft. I am truly the luckiest lady to have you all beside me.

Special mention to my very long suffering mum who goes above and beyond endlessly to make my chaotic day-to-day run smoothly. Nothing would happen without her

And lastly to James, for eating everything, only very occasionally doing the washing up, and supporting me during the highs and lows. What a joy to eat dinner with you every night.

Published in 2022 by Hardie Grant Books,
an imprint of Hardie Grant Publishing
Hardie Grant Books (London)
5th & 6th Floors
52–54 Southwark Street
London, SE1 1UN

Hardie Grant Books (Melbourne)
Building 1, 658 Church Street
Richmond, Victoria 3121
hardiegrantbooks.com

British Library Cataloguing-in-Publication Data. A catalogue
record for this book is available from the British Library.

ISBN: 978-1-78488-527-4

10 9 8 7 6 5 4 3 2

Publishing Director: Kajal Mistry
Senior Editor: Chelsea Edwards
Copyeditor: Emily Preece-Morrison
Proofreader: Laura Nickoll
Indexer: Vanessa Bird
Production Controller: Lisa Fiske
Colour reproduction by p2d
Printed and bound in China by Leo Paper Products Ltd.